The Stranger on the Bridge

The Stranger on the Bridge
My journey from suicidal despair to hope
Jonny Benjamin

and Britt Pflüger

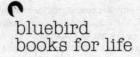

bluebird
books for life

This edition first published 2019 by Bluebird
First published in the UK 2018 by Bluebird
an imprint of Pan Macmillan
20 New Wharf Road, London N1 9RR
Associated companies throughout the world
www.panmacmillan.com

ISBN 978-1-5098-4643-6

1 3 5 7 9 8 6 4 2

A CIP catalogue record for this book is available from the British Library.

Printed and bound by CPI Group (UK) Ltd, Croydon, CR0 4YY

Visit **www.panmacmillan.com** to read more about all our books
and to buy them. You will also find features, author interviews and
news of any author events, and you can sign up for e-newsletters
so that you're always first to hear about our new releases.

I first met Jonny, along with Neil – the 'Stranger on the Bridge' - in 2016 when we sat overlooking the River Thames at Waterloo. We talked about the desperate day that brought them both together, and Jonny's brave journey since then to raise awareness of what it is like to live with mental illness.

As an award-winning campaigner, Jonny is passionate about tackling the stigma surrounding mental health and supporting people to have the conversation about how they are feeling, without fear or prejudice. Mental health is not a dirty word – we all have mental health like we do physical health, good or ill. But I have seen time and again how not seeking help when it all seems too much can impact the rest of our lives. As you will read in this book, at times for Jonny it has been hard but thanks to a strong support network and his personal determination to get through, he provides an extraordinary example to us all.

On the several occasions we have met throughout The Royal Foundation's Heads Together campaign I have been struck not only by Jonny's honesty and openness but his ability to show that a mental health diagnosis should not put limitations upon anyone. With Neil, I watched him run the London Marathon past that very same bridge where their journey began, and I know there is so much more on this journey to come.

For

All my family, friends, and everybody who has shown me so much love and support in every step of my journey. I wouldn't be where I am today without you.

Neil, for stopping that day and giving me the hope I needed to carry on living. And for later meeting me again and joining this adventure we are now on together!

Mum and Dad, who together have been my rock. Thank you for never giving up on me even when I had given up on myself. Please don't blame yourselves for a single thing that happened to me. But instead take heart that your love kept me alive through so many of my darkest hours, and beyond.

And for all of those who think they are unable to overcome their difficulties, I hope this book will instil a seed of hope in you, like the one Neil gave to me when I most needed it.

The Edge of Waterloo Bridge

Standing on the edge of Waterloo Bridge,
With a cold wind cutting my face,
I glance down to the Thames far below,
It ebbs and flows, a sea of waste.
I hold tight to an iron bar behind me,
Fix my gaze on the hands of Big Ben,
Behind me the busy morning commute,
As chimes strike a quarter to ten.
From here heaven feels so close,
My madness dosed with urge,
London sits majestic in its sphere,
As my feet inch off the verge.
Then, abruptly, a voice behind me –
'Hi there, my name is Mike.'
I pretend not to hear but he carries on,
'Whatever it is, it isn't worth your life.'
Mute, I turn to meet the face
Of a man barely older than myself.
Smiling gently, he says with sincerity,
'You will get through this mate, I can help.'
Mike's voice is calm, mine sounds so weak,
As I speak, I begin to cry:
'I don't know what I'm doing any more.'
I was so certain I wanted to die.
But as we converse, me and Mike,
This need is starting to lessen.
His words of hope give me reassurance,

Lift the fog of my depression.
Heavy rain is beginning to fall.
'We could go for a coffee,' he suggests, 'talk it over?'
Mike holds out a hand,
Takes a careful step closer.
I take his hand, he grasps mine tight,
'You'll learn how to cope,'
He says as I climb to safety,
Around me he places his coat.
Three police from behind us charge:
'Are You Hurt?' 'What's Your Name?'
Afraid, I turn and attempt to run;
To the ground I am quickly restrained.
An ambulance arrives into which I am led,
Mike gradually fades from sight.
Dazed by the faces surrounding me,
My vision bleaches to white.
When I awake, I find myself here,
Sectioned on a psychiatric ward.
Finally, I gain a sense so long been removed;
My faith in life, thanks to Mike, is restored.

Jonny Benjamin,

Pill After Pill: Poems from a Schizophrenic Mind

1

On the Bridge

Sunday 13 January 2008

I can't stay in this place.
But I can't stay at home. I'm just going insane.
Why can't they just declare me insane? That's what I am.
G-d, why on earth did you put me here? My mind won't
be still. Why give me this brain? This pained and agitated
brain? I'm back at square one, in the mess I came in.

Take out these veins of mine,
And stop the blood flow to my head,
Then maybe all the voices will go to sleep,
And I will fall into my bed.

Diary entry, 13 January 2008

ON A GLOOMY, DRIZZLY winter morning in January 2008, I found
myself standing on the edge of Waterloo Bridge, determined to end
my life. I had hatched a detailed plan the night before and travelled to the busy commuter bridge at the first opportunity. It was
a mind-numbingly normal hospital morning: woken up at 7 for
meds. Saw psychiatrist at 7.30. Breakfast at 8. Straight afterwards,
I told the nurse on duty that I, a non-smoker, needed to go outside
for a cigarette. As soon as she let me out of the secure door into

the grounds, I ran as fast as I could to the station and jumped on the first train up to London. And then headed to Waterloo Bridge.

Most of my memories of that day are hazy. Many have been pieced together years later. But what I remember most is the overwhelming, desperate need to find peace, and my conviction that the bridge was my only way out. Anything to stop that pain, a pain so intense and unbearable that it left no room for any thoughts beyond the need to end it. Somewhere through the thick fog of my despair, I remember thinking that I didn't want my family to feel guilty. But equally, I didn't want to admit to anyone how I was really feeling, or to see their faces and their reactions when I told them that I didn't want to live any more.

Even though it was a bitterly cold day, I was wearing only a T-shirt and jeans. For some reason, I'd torn out some pages from my diary and wrapped them up in my hoodie, which I then discarded in a public bin. I'll never know exactly what was in those pages, but I clearly didn't want anyone to see them. I'm fairly certain I'd written about my sexuality. I was desperate to end my life with everyone believing I was heterosexual because, amongst all my other problems, I was too ashamed to reveal that I was gay.

On any given day, tens of thousands of people cross Waterloo Bridge, a major artery connecting London's bustling West End with the South Bank. Even if I had known this statistic, it would have meant nothing to me on that dark, freezing January morning. As I walked to the middle of the bridge, stepped over the barrier and stood on the edge, I was oblivious to the stream of commuters walking past me. And in turn, the commuters were seemingly oblivious to the man teetering on the edge – all except for one.

'Why are you sitting on the bridge?' A male voice. I hadn't seen him coming up behind me.

I told him straight away that I was going to jump. And to go away:

'Don't come so close.'

I said this over and over again, not really listening to what he was saying, until he asked me where I was from. It turned out that we'd grown up in the same area of northwest London, and for some reason this made me feel more comfortable talking to him. He started telling me more about himself; he said that he worked as a personal trainer in Covent Garden. He told me not to feel embarrassed about what I was going through, and this gave me permission to begin to open up. He also said he would cancel his clients for the morning and instead we could go somewhere and talk. I was so touched by this that I confided in him that I had run away from hospital that morning, after having been diagnosed with schizophrenia the month before.

When I told him how I was feeling – that until then I hadn't realized I was ill, that I'd thought everyone heard voices in their heads, that I had come to the conclusion that I was possessed by the devil – it was the first time I'd ever opened up so frankly. Somehow I felt safe with this stranger. There was no judgement there. Just compassion.

The turning point came when he said to me, gently but directly: 'I really believe you're going to get better, mate.'

Having this complete stranger put some faith in me, at a point when I had absolutely none left in myself, changed my mind about what I was about to do. Someone believed in me. It restored my trust in humanity.

The last thing I remember the stranger saying was, 'Let's go for a coffee then', as I asked him to help me back over the railings to the pavement. Then suddenly we were intercepted by the police who had been waiting behind me on the bridge in their car, with an ambulance behind them. As soon as I saw them coming towards me, I tried to scramble back over the railings. I didn't want to go with them; I wanted to be with the stranger. I'd felt safe with him. He grabbed me just in time, but then the police stepped in. Ignoring my extreme distress, they handcuffed me and put me in the back of their car. Eventually I was moved into the ambulance and driven to St Thomas' Hospital, where I was sectioned.

I was twenty. Little did I know then that this was the beginning of my road to recovery; a stony, winding one at times, but one which would take me on an extraordinary adventure, and would eventually involve a quest to discover the identity of the mysterious stranger on the bridge.

2

Early Childhood

My name is Jonathan Benjamin.

I was born at Watford General Hospital on 31 January (Saturday) 1987 at 11.56 a.m., weighing 8lb 1oz.

My mother says I used to cry a lot when I was a baby. She also says she could not put me to sleep when I was young, although I can never remember that.

I live with her and my father in north London. I have a brother but he is much older and lives in Manchester where he is at university.

My primary school was an all-boys school near to my house and now I go to a school in Camden Town for Jewish pupils.

At school I always try my best although my temper is hard to control. I haven't got too many friends, I am quite shy. I sometimes get lonely.

I am also a serious and sometimes emotional person but I usually enjoy what I do, as well as being independent and bossy. My favourite thing to do is to watch television, especially *EastEnders*. I'd love to be in *EastEnders* in the future. I think I could also be a pop star! When I'm older I'd like to be like Queen Elizabeth I. She is my favourite queen. She was powerful and determined, which is what I want to be. Her time must have been glorious. I would like to have been around in those years.

Autobiography, written as a school assignment at the age of eleven

JUST BEFORE I STARTED primary school, a well-meaning family friend brought around a video of the original *BFG* movie in which the 'friendly giant', unlike his child-eating peers, blows pleasant dreams into the bedrooms of children via a trumpet. One night he decides to carry a young girl, Sophie, back to his homeland, Giant Country, in order to save her from the cantankerous Mrs Clonkers and her orphanage.

So far, so benevolent. Roald Dahl's Big Friendly Giant, with his enormous nose, bushy eyebrows, jutting chin and bulging eyes, continues to mesmerize and enchant children to this day, most recently in Steven Spielberg's blockbuster film of the book. Yet to my four-year-old self, there was something so haunting and frightening about this giant that he began to invade not only my dreams, but my waking hours too. I dreaded going to sleep, convinced that I could hear his footsteps on the stairs. I would scream and pull the duvet over my head, trying to shut out the horrifying images of the giant who was surely about to steal me away from my parents' house.

I refused to sleep in my own bed and insisted on getting into my mum and dad's instead, and even when I finally returned to my own bedroom, the lights had to be kept on all night. Although I didn't make the connection until much later, the Big 'Friendly' Giant did an awful lot more than just haunt my nightmares, as the adults assumed. Every time I left my room to crawl into my parents' bed, when I turned around, I actually *saw* hooded figures, waiting to snatch me.

Knowing what I know now, these weren't just night terrors but my first hallucinations. But how could I have known that at the age of five?

After months of refusing to sleep in my own bed, my mum decided to seek professional help for me. I started to see a child psychologist, but no real progress was made. Yes, I behaved marginally better, but only because I was afraid of the psychologist, whom I remember as an elderly lady with salt-and-pepper hair. I guess I didn't have the right words to explain my fears and feelings to her. The truth was that I felt unsafe in the world and would act out in fear. My behaviour became erratic, and occasionally even violent and destructive. Although I was hard working and academic at school and my reports were always very good, outside the classroom it was a different story.

One of my earliest memories is of me breaking all of my mum's new jewellery just before my brother's Bar Mitzvah. Another time, I purposefully slammed my dad's hand in a door. On a different occasion, I secretly fed an imaginary Pooh Bear honey in our kitchen, covering the entire room in a sticky mess. One particular incident, which to this day makes me blush with embarrassment and guilt, took place during a visit to my best friend Jamie's house. Jamie's parents had just redecorated his entire room – a big deal to a six year old. A brand-new carpet, freshly painted walls, the lot. There was even a sink with a cabinet underneath which contained, amongst other things, toothpaste and bleach. These proved all too tempting: I managed to destroy the entire room with them. Later I blamed 'Bunji', a purple gremlin I had found in a cereal packet, a destructive and naughty boy who I was convinced was solely responsible for the damage. To this day, I still feel pangs of shame remembering this, especially as Jamie refused to 'dob me in it' and took the blame for it all himself.

I've often asked myself whether I acted out when I wasn't the centre of attention. I was certainly a bundle of contradictions as a child: even though frequently flamboyant and dramatic (I loved wearing my aunt's earrings and showing them off to great effect),

I would often burst into tears at the slightest things. As early as I can remember, my flamboyance alternated with episodes when I felt painfully shy. At the age of three, I wet myself in the Jewish nursery because I was too shy to raise my hand, and although my parents were very sociable and outgoing, I would hide behind my mum when meeting strangers.

Another significant early memory is of the time I was five and I got into trouble with the Sunday School teacher at our local synagogue for drawing a picture of God in class, complete with a sky-blue cloak, wizard's hat, and mask. Any depictions of God are seen as idolatry in the Jewish faith, and therefore forbidden. One of my classmates loudly asked, 'Is Jonny going to hell?' Just then, the bell rang and we all packed our bags to leave. Afterwards, I headed home, crying into my sleeve. As soon as I got in, I ran to my room, knelt down and prayed for forgiveness.

As well as being shy and sensitive, I continued to burst into tears for many years over things which no doubt my peers would have found entirely insignificant. My school was very sports-oriented, and whereas my dad and older brother were big football fans, I struggled to muster any enthusiasm for sports and spent a lot of time alone in the library. In short, I didn't fit in.

However, I did discover an outlet for my artistic personality when, at the age of six, my mum sent me to a local drama school. Finally I was able to express myself. And I flourished. My interests were still a bit different from those of my peers: whilst they were keen to play cowboys and Indians, I wanted to play kiss chase, and I always insisted on being the mummy when acting out 'mummies and daddies'. Around the same time, I also became obsessed with Queen Elizabeth I and the family trees of the Tudors, so much so that I began to draw up elaborate family trees, not just for the Tudors, but also for inanimate objects such as my toys.

I can't remember if I ever made up a family tree for Bunji, but if I did I'm sure it would have been chock-a-block with vandals.

3

Early Signs

from I Am But a Shadow

There's no sound but the humming
Of the voices in my head. I wish I was dead.

Jonny Benjamin, *Pill After Pill*

AT THE AGE OF nine, my world fell apart when my paternal grandmother Estelle passed away. This was my first experience of grief, and it was particularly hard because I had been very close to her. She and my grandfather had got divorced in the mid-1950s, something which was almost unheard of in the Jewish community at that time, and my dad, who was nearly a teenager by then, stayed with his father, who eventually remarried. Estelle, who was stunningly beautiful, almost like a 1920s film star, remained on her own for the rest of her life. My brother Elliot and I spent much of our time with either her or my grandfather's second wife.

Estelle would often come and stay at our house and babysit, and every January she took me to see *Disney's World on Ice*, a much-cherished ritual. With hindsight, I realize that as a divorcée she would have been almost an outcast in the Jewish community, but she was funny, warm and kind; very much like my dad. She also smoked like a chimney, which not only explained her gravelly voice but sadly hastened her death. When she was found dead in her flat as the result of a blood clot, it was so sudden that none of us was prepared for it, least of all me.

It was January, and we had been due to go to the ice-skating show as usual. Instead, in accordance with Jewish tradition, my parents found themselves organizing a swift funeral and sitting shivah in our home – mourning my beloved grandmother while receiving visitors. I didn't understand why all these people were coming round, and why I had to stay in my room during evening prayers, which were reserved for the adults. It was the first time I'd had to deal with death, and I was in shock.

However, I struggled with my emotions in secret. Then, a few months after her death, I began to hear what I thought was the voice of an angel. It was male, and friendly, and initially it was purely observational and quite mundane, pointing out, for instance, that it was 'cold today'. With hindsight, I believe that this particular delusion had a lot to do with my grandmother's death. But it was also probably because I had become obsessed with the Bible: somebody had given me an illustrated children's Bible and, already fascinated by religion, I used to look at it all the time, mesmerized. I became convinced that I must be a very good boy indeed if I was able to hear the voice of an angel.

However, during my last year at primary school, I started to feel increasingly anxious around people and began to bunk off. Then the voice became more troubling. It would tell me off, in an authoritative tone: 'You're in trouble now', and give a running commentary on everything I did. Sounding a lot like Richard Burton, it became the demanding voice of my conscience. At the time, I thought everyone had this voice in their head. I did once talk to my friend about it, but he just laughed and immediately told his brother, who in turn told my mother. When she picked me up from their house, I was so embarrassed that I refused to come downstairs. And I still secretly believed that everyone else was just bluffing and they were really hearing voices too.

Entering the Jewish Free School in Camden was also a huge shock to the system. Before, there had been about thirty pupils in my year, and now there were 250. Although very academic – drama and English were my favourite subjects – I was overwhelmed by the enormity of the school and felt incredibly small compared to the sixth-formers.

I felt so confused about so much 'stuff'. I had so many questions, but no answers. I hated everything about growing up: puberty (did I smell bad? I put on deodorant and chewed a lot of gum, but the thought was driving me nuts), school, love, friends, fights; you name it, I hated it. I felt that my communication skills were poor, especially with adults, and to make matters worse, I kept getting embarrassed and blushing. And I always seemed to be sweating, too. I felt constantly in a bad mood, craving attention. What was wrong with me? I was confused, pissed off about life. Me, my appearance, my voice, the way I did things; always worrying, trying to imagine a mirror in front of me.

On 22 October 2001, aged 14, I wrote:

I can't take any more of school. Too much pressure. I just want to change. Become an actor. Remind me never to complain when I am. School is too hard – I'm going to fail GCSE maths. Hate myself, attitude, looks – especially my spots. Basically got teenage probs.

Two months later, if anything, my turmoil was even worse. And the first signs of my self-destructive urges were starting to emerge:

I felt bad tonight. I hit myself, sprayed gasses on my skin to give me rashes, shaved my skin till my spots bled. I felt insane. Nothing is going right. I've got so much coursework to do and I'm going to fail my GCSEs if I don't improve. Now to calm down. Radio 4's *Poetry Please*. It helps.

A while earlier, I had been to see *The Truman Show* with my best friend. The story of Truman Burbank, the unwitting star of his own reality show, whose every move was picked up by thousands of cameras, had a huge impact on me. I still remember vividly coming out of the cinema and walking to the bus stop with my friend, both of us deep in thought. On the bus home, my friend joked that I could be in my own version of *The Truman Show*: 'There could be cameras on us right now, and the film could have been put on as a bluff.'

His innocent remark would have a long-lasting effect on me. As soon as I got home, I started looking for cameras. Could I really be on *The Truman Show*? The fantasy quickly became my daily reality as I went about identifying where the cameras were hidden: in the mirror, the clock and the light in my room. Every time we went on a family holiday, I was convinced we were on a television set and that the hotel staff and everyone else we encountered were actors. In my mind, there were cameras everywhere.

Rather than being terrified, to a large extent I liked it all. Truman was popular, well respected, and had a good family and friends around him. If I were like him, surely the same applied to me?

Aware of some of this, my friend used to play up to my fantasy. For instance, every time we drank a Coke, he would angle it towards 'the camera', as if it was part of the 'product placement', just like in the film. Although I pretended to laugh this off, I took it very seriously. No doubt this was fuelled by the interest in acting which had started when my mother enrolled me in acting classes at the age of six: I loved performance, and now I was performing around the clock (even if that performance was mainly in my head). I even came up with a monthly magazine about my show, with a picture of myself on the front cover. Everyday coincidences, such as bumping into someone I had thought of earlier that day, took on new meaning and became living proof that I was starring in my own show, and that this chance meeting had been set up by the producers.

'*The Truman Show* Delusion', or 'Truman Syndrome', was first identified by doctors and brothers Joel and Ian Gold. Joel, who is on the psychiatric faculty at New York's Bellevue Hospital and serves as Clinical Associate Professor of Psychiatry at New York University's School of Medicine, came across several patients displaying similar symptoms. These patients all believed themselves to be characters in their own reality TV show after the movie came out in 1998, thus giving rise to the disorder's name. Other psychiatrists maintain that the idea that more people are becoming delusional due to reality TV or '*The Truman Show* phenomenon' is tenuous, and that it is more than likely that these patients would have developed psychoses with or without these influences.

Whatever the case may be, or whatever label one might choose, my own personal '*Truman Show* Delusion' continued until I was twenty, and whilst I kept it a secret, I was happy enough in my own fantasy world and didn't want it to stop.

4

Shame

from Reflection

> Looked into the mirror,
> What did I see?
> I looked into the mirror,
> But I couldn't see me.

> Jonny Benjamin,
> song written at the age of sixteen

IN MY MID-TEENS, WHILE still believing I was starring in my very own version of *The Truman Show*, I developed quite severe acne. Although I kept going to my GP and trying various creams and ointments, nothing seemed to help. On the contrary, the condition got progressively worse. I remember a fellow pupil passing me in the hall one day and commenting, 'Oh my God, you could do dot-to-dot on your face.' Needless to say, his words stung, and as a last resort I agreed to take the drug Roaccutane. This was a well-known acne treatment that unfortunately has been linked to depression and even suicides. Desperate for my skin to clear up, and with no reason to think that they might affect me, I didn't care about possible side effects.

Finally my skin was clear, but instead of feeling better I found myself struggling with low moods. I felt deflated and unhappy without understanding why. At this point I didn't have a concept of what depression was – we had certainly never discussed it at school. When I started to sleep and eat more and more, everyone just put it down to me 'being a teenager'. I also became extremely tearful again: the smallest thing could set me off. Sometimes there wasn't even a 'thing'.

The fact that I hit puberty quite early compared to my classmates didn't help – in fact, I found it really embarrassing. The night before PE, I used to cut the hair on my legs with scissors, wrapping the hairs into pieces of paper which I would secretly throw into a public bin the following day. I was desperate not to be different from the other boys in my year, none of whom had started to get hairy legs yet. I felt so self-conscious in the changing rooms. Cutting the hair on my legs each week made me feel better, although it took ages to do at night. Unfortunately, I didn't realize that cutting only made the hair grow back more noticeably.

It's worth noting that I have *very* hairy legs, something I actually like now. But back then I was embarrassed. What was happening to me? To add to the pressure, I was taking my GCSEs around that time and my grades were expected to be high. But it never would have occurred to me to tell anyone that I was finding things hard. I opted to suffer in silence instead.

It was around this time that the voice in my head changed again, from giving a commentary to one of a more threatening character. Now it was challenging me to do things in threes, such as, 'Pick up the mug three times. If you don't do it, your dad will be hit by a car and killed.' This wasn't just a thought popping into my head. It was an actual auditory hallucination, which sounded no different from a real person talking to me. I came to name this voice 'Shush Shush', as this is what I said back to it when it became too loud.

That year on Yom Kippur, the Day of Repentance, when – according to Jewish tradition – we spend all day in synagogue and fast, the rabbi mentioned in his sermon that it was a sin to be attracted to someone of the same sex. As I sat in synagogue, already tortured by the belief that the voice in my head had become the devil and was bullying me, I felt waves of guilt and shame wash over me. I didn't want anyone to know that I was attracted to boys. Heavily influenced by my faith, desperate to be a good Jew and also highly suggestible, I felt as though I had sinned.

I had for some time been struggling to accept my sexuality. The first time I suspected that I was gay was when I was in a fish-and-chip restaurant for a family birthday and I found myself physically attracted to the waiter who was serving us. This feeling was immediately followed by shame, as religious guilt took over. *Please, this cannot be happening.* And, *You need to get rid of this, this needs to be buried.*

Despite my burgeoning (and buried) feelings for men, I was still attracted to females and liked the idea of being in a relationship, albeit in a platonic way. I had girlfriends, but things never progressed beyond kissing. One girlfriend said to me, 'You're very flamboyant, aren't you?' Not long before that, I remember dancing to 'Crocodile Rock' by Elton John at a cousin's wedding. Everyone was watching me in the middle of the dance floor, camp as can be, and I thought, *Oh no, I need to straighten up.*

Being told at synagogue that homosexuality was a sin was very hard for me. We are of the 'Reform' sect of the faith so, whilst not observant, religion was, and still is, something of strong importance for us. I went to a Jewish nursery school at our synagogue, across the road from our house, before going to Sunday School each week. This is where we learned the Hebrew language and did Jewish studies. Growing up, I also attended synagogue every Sabbath morning, something that is required of you in the run-up to your Bar Mitzvah, and I attended a Jewish secondary school. All in all, it's safe to say religion was a huge element of my youth.

Faith has also always been something that has connected me to my family – not just my parents, but my extended family: celebrating the Sabbath every Friday night with a family dinner, and all the many festivals throughout the Jewish calendar, tied me strongly to them. And although religion was never forced on me – it was my choice to follow it growing up – faith has always meant a lot to my parents, especially my dad, who lost members of his family in the Holocaust. I think my parents have a deep sense of loyalty to Judaism because of this, and as a child and teenager I tried to follow all the rules closely and prayed every night. Homosexuality just wasn't an 'option'.

Nevertheless, at fourteen, I had my first wet dream, about a guy called Joe touching me. When I woke up, at first I thought I'd wet the bed. Shocked, I wrote in my diary that it was 'bad': *I never want another one ever again.*

Surely I was a bad person, and that was why God was punishing me with the voice.

from The Devil's in me to Dwell

I speak in words unheard of by the ear,
And even to my own the sound is veered
To the corner where he sits; the master in my mind;
The man who controls every edge of me, serving his time.

Master in my mind said he was an angel at first,
But later he confessed he was sent as a curse.
An offspring of Satan, a prologue to hell;
Life or death, the devil's in me to dwell.

Jonny Benjamin, *Pill After Pill*

18

To add to my confusion, that year, on the last day of term, we watched *One Flew Over the Cuckoo's Nest*. This was arguably the extent of our mental-health education. Afterwards, I was so shell-shocked I spent the entire breaktime in the toilets. So much about the characters had resonated with me, and what I took away from the film was that I had to be careful not to be like them, otherwise I would end up in a place like that.

But my compulsion to do the things the voice told me continued, as did my low mood. Even from my early teenage years, I'd felt compelled to do certain things, such as pray every time I saw an ambulance or heard a siren. I would say, 'Please God, please let that person be OK.' I don't know where or why it started, but I *had* to say a prayer every time it happened, which, living in London, was tricky to say the least.

The truth was that I was under a great deal of internal pressure and eventually my friendships started to suffer. Around this time, I went on holiday with my best friend, but we argued so much that I ended up calling my parents in tears, asking them to bring me home. I couldn't believe it. My dream holiday, the one I had planned for so many months – how did it all go so wrong? I was devastated. This was meant to have been the best summer ever but now I felt I had lost my best friend.

I was consumed by self-doubts. Not growing up with a natural sense of humour, I was convinced that everyone else was much funnier than me. And then there was my obsession with Madonna. Oh boy, was I obsessed! At one point, I was so infatuated that I cut out every single magazine article about her I could find. But I didn't want to tell anyone; I was afraid it might make them question my sexuality. I even hid all her albums from the display in my bedroom. But, secretly, her music and lyrics spoke to me in a way no other artist's had before. There was one particular song called

'Live to Tell', which felt as if it had been written about my life. It was about hiding secrets – something I did so well in my teens.

At the same time, I had a desire to be 'remembered'. When I was sixteen, I wrote:

> I don't want to be another grave in the ground,
> I want to be somebody when I'm not around.

More than anything, I always wanted to be a singer. I used to get angry at myself for not being able to sing. There's something about music that has always made it the most important medium for me. Whenever I struggled, music was always there to get me through; it was unlike anything else.

My only other distraction was my studies, and despite everything that was going on inside me at the time, I did achieve high marks. However, around the time I moved into the sixth form, my best friend, David, started to notice that I was changing. He started to question why I had stopped smiling and always seemed unhappy. And moody. At some point I had a huge argument with him, then texted him saying I was going to slit my wrists. I didn't know what had come over me: I was so scared of losing him. He was meant to be my best friend but now I thought he was getting tired of me. This incident made me realize that I hadn't been myself for a long time. I just felt so down. On 17 June 2004 I wrote:

> Just what the fuck am I gonna do? I'm crazy, insane, depressed, deluded, out of control, suicidal, no future – FUCK.
>
> I'm ashamed to say this but I keep hiding in the toilets, I can't bear to be around people, I need to be alone.
>
> I think I've got to face facts. I'm depressed. I mean seriously. I need help. The past few days I haven't stopped crying, feeling

so low and even suicidal. I've ignored it for too long. I've got to see someone about it.

In the end David confided in his dad, and they decided that I needed to see a doctor. I guessed I didn't have a choice. I was seventeen and terrified about what was going to happen to me.

5

Doctors

WITH HINDSIGHT, MY REFUSAL to confide in my parents was mis-judged, of course, but – at the time – discussing my problems with them simply didn't seem to be an option. In general, mental illness was not talked about back then, and I had already become so good at hiding mine. There's a real sense of pride within the Jewish community. I didn't want to take that away from my family with the revelation of my mental illness. Or my sexuality.

Growing up, I looked up to my parents; they were so well loved by people. My dad is a successful businessman and my mum is kind of a social butterfly. When things started to go wrong for me, I was sure I was going to damage their reputation, simply because of the stigma surrounding mental illness and homosexuality. I was convinced that people would reject not only me, but my parents too. I didn't want them to have to tell family friends that I was not only mentally ill, but gay, too.

As awful as this sounds, back then I often wished I had been cursed with a physical illness, like cancer, rather than what was happening to me. At least then, I said to myself, people would still love and accept me.

A few days before the appointment that David's father had arranged, I went up to town, alone, to Westminster Bridge. I was unsure what I was going to do when I got there but I can remember thinking that I should have been happy, but I was not. I hated life. This was when I first had the thought that if I was ever going to kill myself, I would jump from that, or another, bridge. That evening, I watched the sun go down over the river and felt peace. But this was just temporary; I needed to find lasting peace so badly.

Luckily, our family GP was very good, and when I went for that first appointment in 2004 he took me seriously. In hindsight, this was a positive start to my journey. He recorded my visits and sent the tapes to CAMHS (the Child and Adolescent Mental Health Services), who put me on their waiting list. Finally, when the day for my first appointment at Northwick Park Hospital in Harrow came, it didn't go according to plan. I got lost but, not wanting people to know that I was going to see a psychiatrist, I couldn't ask anyone for directions. Eventually I arrived, ten minutes late.

A letter which CAMHS sent to my GP afterwards reveals that I was already having suicidal thoughts by then, and that I had even tried to hang myself in the school toilets:

30.7.04

I reviewed Jonathan following an urgent referral from yourself. He described being forced to see you following a bout of being very low in mood. In the last year he has had a number of incidents which he himself finds worrying, such as losing his entire portfolio of artwork on the train and subsequently feeling so bad about it that he tried to hang himself in the toilet. No one was aware of this incident and he managed to keep himself safe until he felt better. It is incidents like this that Jonathan tends to keep ruminating about, which only make him feel a lot worse. Presently there are times when he goes down to the kitchen late at night and removes the kitchen knife from the drawer and holds it against his chest, not quite in an attempt to harm himself, but to be able to feel what it might actually be like to commit this act.

As strange as it sounds, I'd managed to block this incident out of my mind until years later. It happened around the time I was doing my GCSEs. I had spent all weekend working on a school project and had taken it with me on the train that morning – only to leave it behind when I got off. I was so upset when I realized what I'd done that I hung back from my friends, feeling utterly crushed. I got lost in the crowds, fearing that my teacher would not accept my explanation of the truth.

As I started the long walk from Camden Town station to school, thoughts of harming myself and of suicide started to creep in. Already depressed, this felt like the final straw. When I finally arrived at school, I was so angry and upset that instead of going to my first lesson, I went to the toilets and stayed there all morning. I was furious with myself but, above all, I felt worthless. When all these thoughts got too much, I tried to strangle myself. I stopped when the bell rang: it was time for history. 'I needed to get to the lesson. I couldn't miss it.'

CAMHS said that they were concerned, and that they wanted to see me again.

After my first meeting with them, I have a memory of walking in the rain, just feeling numb. On the train home, I travelled up and down the Metropolitan Line for hours, watching the streams of water running down the window, trying to take it all in. I felt empty and scared. I couldn't tell anyone about this, not even my parents. What was I going to do? What would people think? Yet there was also a glimmer of hope now that I would finally get the help I knew I needed.

So I waited. And waited. And waited some more. Finally I received a letter from Northwick Park for my follow-up appointment, for a date four months after my initial one. And with a different doctor. It was all too much; I just gave up. I couldn't go through all that again. My brain felt numb. I couldn't get out the words I wanted to say any more and even when I did they were all mixed up.

But there must have been another part of me that still believed I could get through this on my own, no matter how close I was to giving up. I needed something to aim for and I decided that I should go to study drama at Manchester Metropolitan University, where my brother had studied and had a good time. I thought that maybe I could leave all my baggage behind and turn over a new leaf. I could deal with things myself then, couldn't I?

I was working hard, with my university goal in mind, when something else threw me way off course. Something I have never spoken about before. I was in Pizza Hut with a group of school friends, all male, when the conversation turned to sex and semen, and I mentioned that mine seemed to be a bit of a funny colour – not white, but dark brown (as it later turned out, due to an infection, which cleared up with medication). 'That's weird. You should get it checked out,' one of my friends commented.

So, reluctantly, I told my parents (that was an awkward conversation). Concerned, they agreed that I needed to see a doctor. Eventually I was referred to a urologist and late one afternoon I went to see him with my mum. (Again, awkward.) After asking me a number of questions, the doctor, who must have been in his sixties, turned to my mother and said, 'I want to examine your son. Would you please step out of the room?'

At the time I thought this was weird: the consulting room was huge, and the examination bed at the end of it had a curtain around it. Why did she need to leave? He asked me to get on the bed and pull my pants down. I'd never been so scared. He started feeling around, probing all over with his hands, touching me in ways which felt unnecessary, and wrong. I felt sick. I could hear my heart

25

beating so hard. Then he gave me an ultrasound. Stomach first and then testicles. The whole thing was so horrible I felt about ready to die. Then he told me to lie on my side. He put a glove on and he inserted his hand into my bum. To this day, I can't even begin to describe the enormous fear and the pain. I left the consulting room hot and sweating. My pants were covered in fluid and my bum hurt so much. I spent that evening crying. The whole experience still feels wrong now. Whatever that was – whether there was any wrongdoing on the urologist's part or not – it stayed with me. That was the first time I had been touched intimately, and it was certainly not the way I had imagined it would happen. It haunted me and confused me even more. I didn't want to be touched ever again.

To make matters worse, my maternal grandmother died about this time. She'd been admitted to hospital after a bad fall, and when I visited her, I was horrified by what I saw: it wasn't her. Not the same woman I'd grown up with and loved so dearly. I froze at her bedside when I saw her; she was so weak and so frail. She wouldn't wake. My mum called and called her name, but nothing. I was heartbroken. *Why, G-d? Why prolong the pain?* And my poor mum. How did she manage to stay so strong? I wished I had some of that strength.

My grandma passed away on 23 November 2004. I just couldn't take it in. I'd woken up with intense stomach pains, and then my mum came in and told me. I couldn't stop crying. Mum said, 'Grandma always loved you. She talked about you till the end.' I knew she was at peace, but I was going to miss her so much. I wanted to go back to her flat, drink lemonade, eat her sweets and play cards with her. This would be the first funeral I'd ever been to, and I was so scared.

Around this time, every experience I had seemed to be designed to make me feel like a complete failure: I'd failed three driving tests in the space of a year, failed every single audition for drama school, and I was convinced I was about to fail my A-level exams. Leading up to them, I had begun working part-time in a local café. One day I was taking two bowls of soup over to a couple of women sitting at a table when I tripped and the soup went all over one of their handbags. Fuck. I wished the ground could have opened up in front of me. And then one of the women went ballistic:

'I've only just bought this. You'll have to pay for another one. It's very expensive!'

I almost burst into tears and hid in the kitchen for the next hour. It seemed like breaking point. Afterwards I wrote:

Think I should stay there from now on doing the dishes like I used to. Fuck. My. Life. I'm pretty close to giving up.

In the end, I did pass my A-levels, but as I was really struggling by this point I didn't achieve the results that had been predicted and, being a perfectionist, this was another hard knock. My academic achievements had been not only an escape but my saving grace. I almost cried when I told my mum. She was great, though, and said she was really proud, and so did my dad. But I felt so disappointed in myself.

I had no idea where to go or what to do next.

6

University

from Fake

Fake telephone conversations
Fake you're feeling ill,
Fake the smile upon your face,
But you shall wear it still.
You faked another night out,
Told your friends another lie.
But you just can't tell them
Of the truth, you'd rather die.
So you falsify your whole life,
And exist as someone else.
You
You never know yourself.
The truth comes in the morning,
When the dread floods through your veins.
The truth comes like a warning,
And you can't face the day again.

Jonny Benjamin

EVEN THOUGH MY A-LEVEL grades weren't as high as expected, I still managed to get a place to study drama at Manchester Metropolitan University. It was a highly renowned course – alumni included Julie Walters and Steve Coogan – and it was difficult to

28

get into, so I had done well. I had decided that I wanted to be an actor and now I was free from school forever! A new chapter was about to begin, and it was going to change my life for the better, for sure. I felt as though I was being reborn.

Initially, things were great. I was sharing a flat with other first-year students and I loved my independence, being away from home and meeting new people. Up until now, I had almost exclusively socialized with people from the Jewish community, and now I was starting to make friends from other backgrounds.

I arrived on a Saturday feeling like a new person, free of the old demons. This was a fresh start. Sadly, my elation only lasted a few days. By the following Thursday, I couldn't get out of bed. My low mood had returned with a vengeance, and I simply crashed. All I could think was, *Oh no, I haven't left my demons behind at all.* Not wanting my flatmates to know, I feigned a migraine.

From then on everything became a battle. I found university much harder than I had imagined; constantly surrounded by people who insisted on introducing me to yet more people, and faced with a packed timetable. I was overwhelmed but, unlike at home, I couldn't simply hide in my bedroom. Soon I felt the depression coming back. Every morning I'd get up feeling incredibly low. This was supposed to be my new start in Manchester, at university. Everyone else was having the time of their lives, why not me? It was worse than at sixth-form college because I felt as though I constantly had to wear a mask and pretend to be fine, even in social situations that I found unbearable. Sure, the highs were high, but the lows were very low. I felt lost, but kept hoping things would improve. They didn't.

About six weeks into my course, I plucked up the courage to see my student doctor. When I told her how low I was feeling, her response was, 'Best thing to do is eat more fruit and vegetables, exercise more and sleep better.' I came away feeling dismissed.

What was I supposed to do with that advice? Maybe I'd just have to get on with it.

Drinking is not a big part of Jewish culture, but now, along with most of the other first-year students, I began to drink a lot. With hindsight I can see I was self-medicating, but everybody else was doing it, so it didn't seem like a big deal. And admittedly not everything was terrible: I made life-long friends during that first year and have many happy memories. But I continued to struggle in secret, so much so that I went back to the doctor a few months later. This time she prescribed antidepressants and eventually she referred me to a student counsellor.

During these early years at university, I was prescribed various types of antidepressants. None of these managed to address the delusions I was experiencing, or my other problems. My mood would switch out of nowhere: one minute I was having a great night out, the next I would crash and end up hiding in a toilet cubicle or pretending to be speaking on the phone. Finding it hard to make conversation, I started to feel increasingly awkward and self-conscious in social situations, so much so that I even took up smoking: now, if I was struggling I could always go outside to smoke. On one occasion a chap from my year asked, 'Jonny, why do you smoke? You're not even inhaling!' Mortified that I'd been found out, I immediately gave up. Diary entries from around that time reveal my isolation:

All the nights when I've tried to fit in. I'm invisible to the bar-tender. Always the last to get served. And then you stand there by the bar with the others feeling like a fucking idiot. Everyone seems so much more interesting and funny than you. The circle they formed is closed and you're lingering at the back, pretending to text someone. Sometimes pretending to call someone. It's so much easier feeling like you've got some real purpose being there. I go and hide in the cubicle when it all gets too much for me. They don't even notice I've been gone 20/30 minutes. If only they wouldn't notice if I disappeared completely.

During that summer term, I also began to self-harm. By now I had become extremely introverted and insecure and the only time I came to life was on stage. I was painfully aware that compared with everyone else, I was terribly shy – or so it seemed to me then. One day in the university canteen, I was overcome by the sudden urge to cause myself pain and asked a member of staff for a pair of scissors, on the pretext that I needed to cut off a label. I went straight to a toilet cubicle and cut my arms. All I could feel was immense relief. I stayed there for a long time, until eventually I had to return to my lessons.

The soreness lasted for several days. The pain, a reminder that I deserved this, that the anguish would always be there, would return in waves, especially when the cuts came into contact with water or clothes. I felt that it was a fitting punishment. Once or twice I deliberately moved my sleeve so that people could see the cuts, torn between shame and the need for somebody to see that I was in pain, but when a couple of fellow students commented on them, I glossed over the situation, insisting that I was just going through a stressful time with all the university coursework and that I was fine, really.

Around this time I wrote my poem 'Slaughterhouse':

> What use is this life?
> It's a waste of air,
> And no one really cares.
> Inside I'm already dead,
> All it needs now is a blow to the head.

When I returned to London after the summer term, everything seemed reversed: home now felt like a break from university. Catching up with old friends made me feel better, and more relaxed. No one knew that I was on antidepressants: in my mind, there was a stigma attached to them, and I didn't want to tell anyone that I was having problems. Finally able to enjoy life a little again, I stopped cutting myself.

Eventually it was time to return to university, of course. And my second year proved much tougher and more intense than the first. Whereas my housemates' lectures were generally spread out over the week, as drama students our days were packed with wall-to-wall classes, all of them practical.

That winter term, I played the part of a woman, Ruth Snyder, in Sophie Treadwell's play *Machinal*. Set in New York in the 1920s and based on true events, the play tells the story of a woman (Snyder) who was executed for murdering her husband. Something about Ruth resonated with me to the extent that I felt compelled to play her: a victim of her times, she was more or less forced into marriage to a man she found repulsive. Her trial and eventual electrocution on the electric chair fascinated me deeply: surely she'd acted in self-defence? I felt a lot of empathy for her. Later on that year, I also played Hamlet. Again, I couldn't help but empathize with his character as I found parallels between his life and my own. Hamlet's mind seemed tortured, just like mine, and as before I immersed myself fully in the role.

As much as I loved acting and came alive on stage, both socially and behind closed doors I started to drink more heavily. I was becoming increasingly distressed and, by choice, isolated. There was one particularly awful time when I found myself beating my own face in despair, so hard that people later commented on the bruises. Finding it extremely difficult to be around others, I started to go to the woods a lot, to cry in secret. Other times, I would lose my temper over virtually anything – mini-implosions triggered by stress and worry. At one point I went berserk and threw a chair across a room at university, smashing anything in my way. Afterwards, still boiling with anger, I cried. What was I going to do? Where was I going? I wanted to be someone. I didn't want to be this weak idiot any more, walking around constantly asking myself, *Why did I just say that, or do this?* or, *What does that person think of me?* I was so insecure and so paranoid that I never felt at ease or happy. Worst of all, it was all bottled up inside me, and I rarely let it out.

In my first year, for some reason I had taken to walking around the corridors at the Manchester Royal Infirmary, and at times of stress I continued to do this:

Monday 9 January 2006

First day back at uni, wish it was the last.

Started off great – nice to see everyone again, all smiles and hugs.

Then it all went wrong and I ended up so down. I walked to the Royal Infirmary. I don't know why.

So I walked up and down the many long corridors, listening to 'Creep' on repeat.

Then I went to sit in the cold outside – I sat and cried. A cat came out of the bushes and it stood there for ages. Just watching. Maybe it was Grandma! I've got to go the docs. I just feel helpless, despairing, no one has a clue.

Eventually I did start seeing a counsellor. I really opened up to him and even showed him the scars on my arms, but he displayed an alarming lack of empathy. He seemed cold to me, and had zero sense of humour: I just didn't feel as though I was getting anywhere with him.

Despite everything, I was excelling academically. I was the first one there in the morning, and the last one to leave. More than once, fellow students remarked that I was working too hard, but work was my escape from the turmoil in my head.

Nobody knew, but secretly I was still suffering from delusions, and I still believed that I was in *The Truman Show*. I remember a particular time one summer when I was thinking about a student from my first year, and suddenly – wouldn't you know it? – there he was. I bumped right into him. Surely this couldn't be a coincidence? I was convinced that this was a sign that 'they' knew what I was thinking, that 'they' had a plan for me and had planted him there.

7

Back to Black

DURING THE WINTER TERM of my third year at university, in 2007, I performed in two plays, for the first time in front of the public. The first one was *Victory* by Howard Barker, in many ways a rather strange play set in post-Cromwellian England and brimming with frivolity, sex and corruption in the aftermath of the restrictions imposed during the Puritan era.

The second was *After Mrs Rochester* by Polly Teale, based on the troubled life of the writer Jean Rhys and her 1966 novel *Wide Sargasso Sea*. Although it only had a small cast, I played several roles. Again, I immersed myself fully in the story, which I felt mirrored my own life, with its running theme of mental health, as Rhys finds herself trapped by men into a spiral of self-destruction. This was when I wrote 'I've Got Blues':

> I'm sorry,
> For the state that I am in.
> And I'm sorry,
> I just could not let you in.
> But now I need you,
> Like I need to die,
> And I'd rather be with you,
> Than have to say goodbye.
> Don't leave me to die.
> Don't leave me,

In my mess,
In my blood, my sick, my tears.
This time I need somebody,
There I've said it,
I can't do it,
On my own any more,
Please don't leave me,
At least pick me up from the floor.
I don't want to see another doctor,
I can't bear to swallow another pill,
I don't want to cut my arms any more.
I need someone to understand,
Somebody to tell me it will be ok,
I need a friend to hold my hand.
Help me, help me, help me,
Don't leave me here to die.

That November 2007, while we were still rehearsing, something happened which plunged me further into despair. One of our classmates, Sarah, had been suffering from cancer, but we all believed that she was getting better. So when I received a phone call on a Sunday morning with the news that she had suddenly passed away, it shocked me to the core. I had spoken to her only a week earlier, in the canteen. I'd sat across the table from her and watched her take her last chemotherapy tablets, convinced she would pull through. As it turned out, she had caught a really bad cold and her weakened immune system simply couldn't fight it off. It was the final straw. Struggling to take it all in, I just couldn't accept the news.

Later that afternoon, I had a car accident. In itself, it was very minor; another driver reversed into me. But coming straight after my friend's death, it triggered something. I felt an acute sense that

I was losing control and couldn't stop crying. As the day went on, I became more and more agitated, dazed with grief, restless and tearful, convinced that I was going mad. I started to drink and even wrote a farewell note before deciding to go for a walk in the dark. Unfortunately, rather than calm me down, walking made me feel even more distressed and I started to speak out loud, anything that came into my head, in a language that almost wasn't my own.

I ended up walking into the middle of a dual carriageway near my student house, screaming and shouting as the cars whizzed past me. I could no longer control what was coming out of my mouth or how I was walking. A few drivers pulled up and stopped on the hard shoulder to ask whether I was OK, but I just shouted at them to leave me alone. It felt like one of the darkest moments of my life.

It was a freezing night, but I walked and walked, cold and angry, for what seemed like hours. Finally I collapsed and found myself lying on the cold ground, sobbing. I realized that I really needed help and summoned up the courage to call one of my housemates: 'I need you to come and get me. I need help. Please!' I managed to tell them where I was. 'I don't know what's going on with me. I'm out of control.'

When Jayne and Tom found me, they were clearly shocked by what they saw. To make matters worse, I resisted when they tried to get me into their car to take me to hospital. More people stopped to help, and eventually I relented. On the journey to Manchester Royal Infirmary, I finally opened up to Jayne and Tom about what had been going on and how bad I'd been feeling. Up until then, I'd still been too proud to let anyone know.

When we arrived at A&E, I was seen by a doctor who may or may not have been a psychiatrist. I was too confused to take in many details, but I do remember that he came across as unsympathetic and cold. Even though I was obviously very agitated and distressed, I was told that they couldn't admit me as they had no beds. I begged him to let me stay: 'I want, no, I *need* to be somewhere safe.' Even when I revealed to him that I was planning to kill myself, he just gave me some Valium and said: 'Take these, and hopefully you'll feel better in the morning.' Later, Jayne revealed to me that he had taken her and Tom to one side in the corridor and asked whether there was any chance that I 'could be putting this on.'

The next day I wrote in my diary:

> They couldn't help me. I need diagnosis, hospital treatment. I give up, trying to get help. No one cares about mental health. So I left at 4 a.m. Back to Black.'

Jayne and Tom took me home and sat with me until I fell asleep. I know it must have been incredibly tough for them, not knowing what to do. The following day they told me that I needed to go home and tell my parents, but I refused: 'I know I should, but I really need to finish this play. Everyone is struggling after Sarah's death.' I kept repeating over and over again that I needed to finish the play. And so I did.

The next few weeks were pure hell but I trudged on. On 10 December I wrote:

> I don't have anything to express any more. I don't know where it's gone. I used to care, I don't any more. I just really want to finish, to die. I just can't see much point to going on. I have nothing to offer. Why even write this any more?
>
> I want to die. And yet I can't bring myself to take an overdose or throw myself off a bridge.

At one point I very nearly gave up. I even wrote a farewell letter:

> I'm so so so sorry. You don't know how much I am. I didn't want this. I tried to stop it. But I've been holding it in for so long now and I can't take it any more. What I'm talking about is a deep depression. I wish I could have told you but I just couldn't cos no one would understand it. I love you all so dearly but I never had the heart to show you who I was so I kept it silent. Well now I can't any more and I'm so ashamed.
>
> I love you all and I'm so sorry to put you through this. I don't know what to say other than sorry. I'm more sorry than I've ever been about anything. But it's not your fault and there's nothing you could have done.
>
> Sorry again.
>
> Love you,
>
> Jonathan xxx

Over the years I've learned that sometimes it is the most mundane things that get through to you in your time of need. In this case it was my housemate coming home and simply saying, 'Come down for some dinner. We'll watch TV.' Funnily enough, we ended up watching *Friends*.

And so I struggled on.

Up until now, the stage had been my escape, a place where I could inhabit other people's minds and lives, but even that no longer worked. At the final dress rehearsal for *After Mrs Roches-ter*, my tutor remarked, 'You're not actually *there*. You're not *in* the play. Where are you?' It was a very apt question.

When my parents came to see me on stage for the first time, they really enjoyed it, but commented afterwards that I looked pale and tired. They've often said since that that was the first time they suspected that something wasn't quite right. Until then, I'd been so good at hiding everything that troubled me, and they'd had no reason to suspect that anything was amiss. I'd never been in trouble, had a lot of friends both at school and at university, and even while I was in Manchester I'd stayed in touch with relatives – my dad's sister lives there, and I would regularly go round to have Friday dinner with her and my uncle. So when my parents mentioned their concerns after the play, I was able to dismiss them, and they decided that I was probably just still shaken up from losing my friend and the car accident. In reality, I was convinced that I had been rubbish on stage, that everyone else had been so much better than me. This was demoralizing: I'd always got a buzz out of acting. I used to feel the adrenalin surging through me, but now there was nothing.

At the wrap party following the final performance in mid-December, I excused myself by saying that I wasn't well, and went home. I had recently signed up to the online dating site Gaydar, and that night I decided to finally meet somebody. I wanted to try it. It didn't take long to find someone who suggested I come to his house and I agreed. I got very drunk once I arrived. The guy wanted to have sex, but I told him that this was my first gay experience and I wasn't ready.

Although this obviously was not what he'd had in mind, we still had a very nice time together. The following morning, however, he calmly suggested that I should leave: 'I need to do some Christmas shopping.'

This was enough to feel like a huge rejection and, when I got home, I had a massive breakdown. Alone in the house because my friends had already left for Christmas, I lay in bed all day crying, watching the same music video over and over again: 'Love Is a Losing Game' by Amy Winehouse.

The previous night had seemed so perfect in every way, just bliss, but when he had told me to go, everything had turned cold and grey. Walking down the street, I had kept my head down, feeling the eyes of everyone around me burning into me. I just wanted to be alone in my bed or, better still, back in the previous night. I'd felt so safe when he held me; when he kissed me time had stopped. It had felt like a very special place, but now it was lost. I didn't understand – he'd been so kind, he'd smiled, as though he cared. I'd suddenly felt complete for the first time, but now I felt deceived:

> I know it was just a one night stand,
> But why can't I let go,
> You know you really must understand,
> I've grown to love you,
> In one night, I know it seems too soon,
> But I need you, I need last night,
> Perhaps this afternoon?
> Please, make it all alright again,
> Is it just a memory then?
> Or is last night just a dream,
> You will never, never know what last night means to me.

That Monday, I drove to London, sobbing all the way. Considering the state I was in, I have no idea how I managed to get home. As soon as I pulled into my parents' driveway, and without even speaking to my mum and dad, I went straight to bed and stayed there for the rest of the day, crying, wanting to die. I had the pills ready, and at one point I even tried to suffocate myself. But then I thought of my mum and dad. Of course they realized that something was wrong. Although I couldn't face telling them that I was suicidal, when I eventually got out of bed the following day I finally admitted that I needed to see a doctor. Luckily, I was able to get an appointment that afternoon. As soon as I saw my GP I burst into tears and told her everything. She then called in my parents.

This is the hardest moment of my life. To have them handed all my problems. All the things for years I've never told them. They were amazing.

My GP managed to find me a bed in a psychiatric hospital in north London, and my parents took me straight there. Unlike Amy Winehouse, I did agree to go to rehab. In the end, I spent a month in hospital, where I was diagnosed with schizophrenia.

8

Suicidal

Suicidal feelings are too difficult to put into words. It's like the feeling is too intense and overwhelming for the intellect.

Diary entry, 13 January 2008

AFTER BEING ADMITTED TO hospital in December 2007, I spent the first few days on a suicide ward. It was dubbed the 'Goldfish Bowl' because it was comprised of four or five single rooms arranged in a circle around the nurses' station. Each room had a large window facing the station, and a staff member sat with the patients at all times. Even when you went to the toilet or took a shower, you had to keep the door open so they could supervise you, and they came to the canteen with you. Zero privacy.

I was allowed to keep my diary, but everything even remotely 'dangerous' had been taken off me, including my headphones, which meant I couldn't even listen to music. I remember lying on my bed all day, staring into space, unable to concentrate on a book or even a magazine. Time seemed to stand still, except for those few hours when my mum and dad visited.

On my first day on the ward, I kept asking myself how I had ended up there. My initial reaction was disbelief. This couldn't be happening to me, surely? Schizophrenics were crazy, dangerous people, like the ones you saw in movies and read about in the tabloids. Like the ones in *One Flew Over the Cuckoo's Nest*. How would I explain my diagnosis to those closest to me? Looking at the pain in my mum's eyes that night was almost too much to bear. How was I ever going to get through this? Sitting on my bed, I felt that I had never been in a darker place:

> AAH, I JUST WANT TO GO CRAZY. I am. I'm not. I need to trust. I need to keep on. Have faith. But it's so hard when you're lost. I should have just killed myself. Why didn't I? I really can't now. I really can't. It's too late.

I was tired. So tired. Minutes felt like hours: minutes when I wished I was dead. There was nothing to do there, and only four other people in the hospital, although the nurses told me it would get busier after Christmas. A peak time for mental illness, it seemed.

Two days later, I dipped even further:

> It's crazy, the highs and the lows. Not that you could call them that. It's more like the lows to the low-lows. During today I went from low to low-low, to low-severe-low. I just had to hurt myself to make it better. I got this rage and began scratching myself. I did the right thing and asked for help and got medication.

And on 23 December:

> So many memories are flooding back to me, and even the ones that were happy now seem sad.
> I want to be a child more than ever.

They dosed me up with antipsychotics and antidepressants, which made me feel constantly drowsy and tired. It was a few days before

I was even able to leave my room and take part in group therapy; although my psychiatrist saw me every morning on his rounds, there was no one-to-one therapy. Group therapy seemed strange to me, and I didn't want to talk. So I remained silent.

On Christmas Eve – I remember clearly that it was a Monday – I was finally moved to my own room, away from the Goldfish Bowl. At last I had some privacy! Now I could pick my nose and fart, and do all the silly things I liked to do and not feel embarrassed. This, and the fact that I would be allowed home for Boxing Day, put me in better spirits.

Sadly, the mood didn't last. On Christmas Day I went downhill again. Where had all my excitement and joy gone? What a sad life to be there on Christmas Day. Unused to my moods swinging from highs to lows and back again, I felt completely at the mercy of them. I was once again trapped in a vicious cycle of self-loathing and self-pity, and not even gifts could bring me joy or make me smile. I wrote a lot of poetry that night. Morbid, depressing poetry, but somehow it helped clear so many thoughts.

As arranged, I went home on Boxing Day. I'd been so looking forward to this, but when it actually happened it felt strangely surreal. Especially so, knowing that I would have to return to the psychiatric ward. So at first I was angry, not just at the situation but at those around me. Looking back, I think I was horrid to everyone. What was the point? Of anything? *Just kill yourself.* I calmed down with time, and by the end of my visit, I would have given anything to have stayed with my mum and dad.

The next few days felt like a very black hole. There was no doubt that 2007 had been the worst year of my life, and the New Year seemed to offer no hope. On 1 January I was moved back to the Goldfish Bowl:

Today I hit a wall. Such a need to kill myself. I would have if you had placed a few bottles of pills in front of me. Now I'm drugged up to the eyeballs, a suicide watch over me.

It's a shame but, I don't know, I'm just crazy, I think.

Now my diagnosis was refined to schizoaffective disorder, a condition that combines aspects of schizophrenia and bipolar disorder. On the face of it, I was finally able to put a name to my delusions, paranoia and mood swings, but 'in reality', whatever that meant to me, I simply didn't want to deal with it. I was stunned; I felt as though I had been given a life sentence there and then. Growing up, everything I had heard about schizophrenia had been negative, frightening even, and invariably implied violence. And now I had to sit there and listen as my parents received my diagnosis. I was utterly mortified.

One of the main reasons why my diagnosis was such a shock to me (and my parents) was the powerful and damaging stigma attached to schizophrenia and schizoaffective disorder. There are so many myths and misconceptions, it's no wonder I thought it was the end of the world, and that I would never get better.

Firstly, contrary to commonly held beliefs, although 'schizo' means 'split', people with schizophrenia do not have a split personality: the split refers to *gaps* (or a splitting) in our ability to think and express emotions. Secondly, many people falsely believe that schizophrenics are dangerous and need to be monitored at all times. This is arguably the most damaging misconception of all, and it is important to educate people that violence is not a symptom of schizophrenia – in fact, people with the illness are far more likely to be victims of violence, rather than the perpetrators.

And yes, some of us – but not all – do hear voices. These auditory hallucinations, which are far more vivid and 'real' than mere thoughts, can have a huge impact on our lives. They tend to torment and taunt us, telling us that we are not good enough, or that bad things will happen to us (in contrast to the stereotype that the voices are urging us to commit terrible acts). The voices are so loud that when we are unwell, we often struggle to block them out while we are having conversations with other people; this is why we can appear distracted. Silencing them all day long is utterly draining, which means that we tire more easily. And then there are the suicidal thoughts, of course. The last time I was suicidal I thought to myself, *One day we'll treat suicidal thoughts like getting a headache. We'll know that they can be treated, and we will no longer be scared of them.*

People suffering from schizoaffective disorder or schizophrenia are also prone to delusions (false beliefs that our minds trick us into clinging on to), and our thoughts and behaviour can be irrational. It seemed that I was almost a textbook case.

Along with coming to terms with this shocking diagnosis, and just to add to my confusion, I was suddenly confronted with the fact that I wasn't the star of my own TV show and that the voice in my head wasn't real. Even despite this, I was still questioning whether that revelation in itself wasn't all part of the show, a set-up, and therefore untrue.

As if all this wasn't enough to deal with, my psychiatrist started pressing me on the issue of my sexuality. But I wasn't ready to talk about it yet. We'd never talked about homosexuality at home. I'd heard it spoken about in school and in synagogue, but only ever in a sinful way. I was terrified of my parents' reaction; in fact, I was more afraid of them knowing about my sexuality than about my mental-health problems. I feared it would bring shame on them within the Jewish community. Mental illness at least seemed a little more acceptable. Although fortunately a lot has changed now, as

Jewish leaders and the media begin to talk about it more openly, homosexuality back then was really frowned upon. Every single man I knew in the Jewish community around us had married a female and set up a family. Every single one of my cousins; all the children of my parents' friends. Everyone. The thought that I would have to do that and live a lie – I can't even begin to describe what that did to me. There only seemed to be one way out.

I think this was why I tore those pages out of my diary, the ones that I'm almost certain were about my sexual encounter with the guy in Manchester, before going to the bridge. Flicking through my diary now, the missing entries seem like a poignant reminder of my shame and confusion over the entire episode.

What's more, on 5 January 2008 I went down even further. I suddenly developed panic attacks for the first time. Up to this point, it had 'just' been depression, but now acute anxiety hit me right in the stomach. It was painful, oh so painful. I couldn't breathe. Now I really felt I couldn't take any more. I started to work out a detailed suicide plan.

As predicted by the nurses, the hospital was completely full now, which felt overwhelming because I had just got used to the patients who were in there with me. Clearly a lot of people were very unwell after Christmas. On 7 January, I realized that I should have been back starting university, yet here I was, feeling a million miles away, not knowing what the future held. At some point I formulated a plan to retire to the Lake District and not talk to anyone, ever again: this seemed like a viable course of action at the time, something to live for. Even though I desperately wished I wasn't feeling so low, I refused to tell anyone just how bad I actually was. I just wanted to get out of there.

That Sunday evening, on 13 January, I couldn't bear it any more. The dread, the anxiety, the fear. I no longer knew what to do. I couldn't stay in that place, but I couldn't stay at home either. I was clearly going insane: *G-d, why on earth did you put me here?*

That night, something suddenly became clear in my mind, like a revelation: I decided to take my own life the following day. *When everything in your mind is a total mess, you finally have an answer.*

To the outside world, I carried on as normal. I even had dinner with the other patients. Only I knew that my plan was finally in place.

9

Rescue

I am but a shadow of my former self,
Since this cancer of the mind took over my health.
I sit each day in my white lilied cell,
Waiting with letters full of lines of farewell.

Jonny Benjamin, *Pill After Pill*

AND SO I FOUND myself, that fateful January morning in 2008, about to jump off Waterloo Bridge. As I described, once the stranger had pulled me back down, I found myself handcuffed and agitated in the back of a police car. One of the officers kept telling me to calm down. Eventually, after they had repeatedly asked for my next of kin, I gave them my parents' phone number.

'Mrs Benjamin, we've got your son with us. He tried to kill himself.'

I heard my mum's scream from the back seat of the car. I can still hear it to this day.

The police took me to a waiting ambulance and I was driven to St Thomas' Hospital. There, they bundled me into a waiting room where I sat in a corner, still handcuffed, a policeman watching me from the other side of the room until my father turned up. Hours later, I was finally assessed by a psychologist who determined that I needed to be sectioned:

> Risk to self – attempted to jump from bridge today. Has described feelings of self-harm which he describes as 'dark thoughts'. Father is present and aware of section 2 assessment. He does not object to Jonathan being detained as he wants the best outcome for his son.

A section 2 meant that I could be admitted for up to twenty-eight days. They asked me whether I wanted to stay at St Thomas' or return to the hospital in north London. As I was already an inpatient at the other hospital, it made sense to go back there.

The rest of my stay there is a bit of a blur, but my psychiatrist eventually lifted the section and I was released from that hospital a few days before my twenty-first birthday. While my school friends and contemporaries were out celebrating the start of their adult lives and independence, my life revolved around the hospital. I still had to return as a day patient for group therapy and this continued for several months.

In the meantime, I was determined to get back into some kind of 'normal' routine, whatever that meant, so when a family friend got me a filing job with an accountancy firm in Great Portland Street, I took it. For months, I was stuck in a basement, surrounded by piles and piles of documents. It felt to me as if I were trapped in some kind of Kafkaesque nightmare. My employers were incredibly sympathetic, but my medication – a combination of antidepressants and Olanzapine, a strong antipsychotic drug – made me so dopey that I often fell asleep by 11 a.m. To make matters worse, I felt so unsettled in life generally; I just couldn't come to terms with what had happened to me. I felt different from before my diagnosis, as though I had lost something. Or, as my psychiatrist put it, 'You are a shadow of your former self.'

Still, at least the devil voice, which had been so loud and intrusive before, was quieter now, and I was no longer under the delusion that I was in *The Truman Show*.

I worked at the filing job until the summer of 2008, when I decided to go back to Manchester Metropolitan University to finish my acting degree. That autumn term, during my final year, I stopped taking my meds. They had made me gain three and a half stone in nine months, and I just couldn't cope. Unfortunately, one of the side effects of suddenly coming off this kind of strong medication can be what are known as 'brain zaps', where you experience what feels like electric shocks to the brain in the form of a deeply unpleasant pulsating sensation, and problems with your vision. From the moment of waking in the morning, I felt disorientated. And frightened. What was happening to me now? Was I having a brain haemorrhage?

This time I ended up in a Manchester hospital. My heart rate was worryingly high, but I didn't confess to the doctors that I had just come off strong medication and they couldn't work out what was wrong with me. In fact, I don't think I even told them about my diagnosis, and of course my records were still at a hospital in London.

A doctor at my GP's surgery later suggested that these side effects might have been delusions related to my schizoaffective disorder. It was only through my own research on the internet that I discovered that other people have experienced these 'brain zaps' too, and that their symptoms – not just an unpleasant feeling but the complete inability to function, the strong urge just to lie down and rest – are a recognized condition.

When I was finally discharged, with the doctors at Manchester still none the wiser, I experienced another side effect of suddenly coming off my meds. I became increasingly delusional, convinced that I was the Messiah, with visions of how I could change the world. Determined to deliver my message, I started writing letters to people in the public eye – singers, actors, the government; you name them, I wrote to them. In these letters I outlined the effects of poverty, disease and hunger, pointing out that, by the end of that day, 26,000 children around the globe would have died, and imploring politicians to raise taxes, highlighting the huge figures these measures could raise in the UK and US alone. And why not force people and businesses to switch off their lights at night? This would not only generate even more money but also save the planet! And why not make more businesses go Fairtrade?

We need to do something, don't we?

I don't want to compare this situation to that of the Holocaust – it's just not right – but what I will say is this: in 1945 when the horror and destruction of the Holocaust was revealed, the world said it wouldn't stand by and watch humanity suffer again.

Over 9 million people died in the six years of the Holocaust.

'Never again,' they said.

Over 9 million children die every year in the Third World.

It's happening again. And what are we going to do about it? Me, I have to do something, anything. I can't lead a normal life, I won't rest, I will do everything I can. You, you can finish reading this letter and return to pretence, or you can join me and save our brothers and sisters. I'm asking for your help to make the Third World, one world.

Thank you for your time.

Kind regards,

Jonny Benjamin

Not trusting the postal service, I hand-delivered every single one of these letters, including one to Elton John's address in Holland

Park, which I had somehow found out. When I got to his house I couldn't find a letterbox, so I shoved it under his garage door. I was also particularly keen to deliver my message to Simon Cowell, so I went to the offices of his record label and left a note at reception.

In addition, I became increasingly concerned about the plight of the homeless population, to the point where I sent another letter, this time to various MPs. It was just as detailed and rambling as the first one:

Last winter in London was the coldest in the capital for over 30 years. Daytime temperatures averaged just 1.5°C, and night-time temperatures fell as low as –6°C.

Despite this, there were over 100 people sleeping rough on the streets of London during that time.

I was born and bred in London. My great-grandparents fled here to escape the persecution they were facing as Jews in their eastern European homes. If this city hadn't welcomed them and allowed them to build a new life here, one can only fear what would have become of them.

For so long I have had nothing but pride for my home town. But then I faced a serious illness and I was forced to reassess the way I see things. Now every time I walk these streets, I am faced with guilt, frustration and confusion. Why is it there are 3,600 people living on the streets? And, more importantly, why aren't we doing more to stop it?'

Needless to say, I never heard anything back. This plunged me into an even deeper depression. I felt dejected, ignored. Why did nobody want to hear what I had to say? I was seething with rage, so angry with the world. But mostly I was angry with myself – for my diagnosis and for everything that had happened in the last few years.

I felt a failure. At some point, when I was at my most unwell, I even devised a plan to drive a car loaded with explosives up to 10 Downing Street. Thankfully I never did it; apart from anything else, I don't think I could have blamed that one on Bunji the purple gremlin.

At around the same time, I became obsessed with the singer and civil-rights campaigner Nina Simone, whose struggles with bipolar disorder and consequent suicide attempt have been well documented. I identified with her so much that I was convinced I was channelling her, to the point where I began to mimic her. I even composed and recorded a song in her honour and sent it to various record labels:

Today I'm Nina Simone,
Tomorrow I'll be Che,
And this is the beautiful mind,
Of a boy called Jonny Ray.
We won't let them take us away.

Now I don't know, no,
What I've done wrong,
All I know is to the devil I do belong.

But every night I said my prayers,
And every month I paid my bills,
And the only life I ever killed was mine, oh mine.

I never ever hurt no man,
I never made my Mama cry,
So why possess me with these thoughts? My schizophrenic mind?

Cut out my veins and blow my brains,
Somebody save me from this pain.
Skin my body, skin my soul,
Somebody help me out this hole.
'Cos I'm just a shadow, I'm just numb.
Somebody kill me, get your gun.

Other female singers with whom I became obsessed in my twenties were Amy Winehouse, Billie Holiday, Dusty Springfield, and Etta James. It was their voices that first attracted me to each of them; they sang with such raw emotion. And then I learned each of their stories, and it broke my heart to discover they had all suffered a great deal in their lives. It's something that plays on my mind to this day. How could all these singers, each with such enormous talent, suffer so much? The deaths of Amy Winehouse, and later Whitney Houston, upset me enormously. People always refer to these singers as 'troubled', something I find frustrating. Their talent was so much bigger and brighter than their troubles! It's the lack of support around them that I believe is really troubled.

All this time, I still didn't admit to anyone about my delusions. And even my psychiatrist didn't know that I was no longer on my meds.

But I was about to reveal another secret: that I was gay.

10

Graduation

I lay down on the Heath,
Let the ground hold my grief.

I watch the sun die,
Burn the clouds in the fading sky.

The crows sing from the treetops,
Savour the flesh below that rots.

The winter wind sweeps through the grass,
The breeze it stings as it rushes past.

And I shut my eyes,
For the last time.

Jonny Benjamin, song from record demo,
written on Hampstead Heath

WHILE I HAD BEEN in hospital, a nurse called Carolina had kept telling me about her son being gay, and how proud she was of him. I was still in deep denial, and it was only later that I realized she was trying to help me come to terms with my own sexuality. After much anxious deliberation, and encouraged by my psychiatrist, I decided to come out to my parents. They still had no inkling. I told my mum first, in the psychiatrist's office. Still reeling from my diagnosis and suicide attempt, she was stunned, lost for words. Eventually we went home, but when it came to telling my dad I was so ashamed that I hid my face in my hands until he told me to take them away, that it was OK.

Despite my parents' fairly positive reaction, I was still finding it hard to accept both my diagnosis and my sexuality. I hadn't even told my brother.

When I went back to Manchester to finish my degree I met a guy, but it proved to be a short-lived romance. He was the first person I'd ever been with, and the relationship moved so quickly that I told him I loved him after four days. We both ended up hurting each other, and really I was in no fit state of mind to be in a relationship. I was still far too unsettled.

About this time, I was due to be an usher at my brother's forth-coming wedding, but my medication had made me gain so much weight that I started to become obsessed with how I would look in the photographs. So much so that in addition to coming off my meds, I began to starve myself.

By now most of my friends had already graduated, and I found myself living by myself in student halls where there were no social areas. Isolation became inevitable. By this time, some of my friends knew of my hospital stays but I still hadn't told them about the meds. In fact, reluctant to discuss my diagnosis, I tended to laugh the whole thing off, pretending it was 'just' depression. I hated uttering the word 'schizophrenia' because of the huge stigma attached to it. A few friends, unaware of my condition and the side effects of my medication, had already commented that I was getting a bit chubbier and, feeling bloated due to the antipsychotics, I became even more determined to lose the weight. Urgently. I became obsessed with taking endless photos of myself with my digital camera to track my progress. Seeing as these were the days before smart phones, this was no mean feat – I had to turn the camera around to get a decent shot. The fact that I was not eating properly was easy to hide now that I was living on my own, with little contact with my fellow students in the halls. It got so bad that I wouldn't leave my room unless I was happy with the way I looked.

Like most people, I love the smell of freshly baked bread, but I developed such a skewed relationship with food that one day I found myself walking past a bakery and feeling nauseated by the aroma wafting out into the street. I had trained my mind to go off food. I started to feel guilty after eating, ashamed and regretful. I hated my own body, and my face in particular. I didn't want people to look at me while I was walking down the street; I wanted people to see me for the things I had inside me. So I focused my eyes on the pavement, avoiding people's gaze, paranoid about what they must think of me. Behind their smiles, were they saying, 'He's not looking his best'? Surely the six-pack billboard men were laughing at what they saw, the passengers in cars pointing at me, people in shops whispering. I wished the ground would open up and swallow me. *Don't look at me.* This body, this face, felt so out of place.

I became obsessed with rice cakes: not only were they low in calories, but they were bland and tasteless, almost a form of self-flagellation. In a similar way, while I wanted to avoid having to look at myself in shop windows, I was also compelled to take a peek, as yet another form of self-punishment. And sometimes I would look in the mirror in the forlorn hope that the weight had fallen off, as if by magic. I later learned that these contradictions are yet another symptom of my condition.

I recently found my diary from around the time my eating disorder kicked in. It reveals the sorry cycle of self-hatred I was stuck in. On 1 December 2008: *I got McDonald's tonight. Fuck the diet. I'm not going to make it anyway. Nobody likes me.* And on 20

December: *I got a curry for tea. I'm putting on so much weight. And here comes Christmas. So more weight will be put on, no doubt.*

As a result of my starvation diet, I looked just fine in the wedding photographs. Unfortunately, this was not an accurate reflection of how I felt. At a traditional Jewish wedding, it is customary for the rabbi to stand up in front of the congregation before 'the veiling of the bride', which is when the groom goes into a room to lift his bride's veil. The rabbi decided to take this opportunity to tell me – and the rest of the synagogue – that he had a daughter who would be perfect for me. This distressed me so much that I ended up sobbing as I walked down the aisle with my grandmother.

As part of my continuing degree course, we had to perform a showcase at the Soho Theatre in London. This included one monologue and one duologue, in front of a live audience and casting directors, and afterwards we were expected to do a meet-and-greet. I somehow managed to get through the performance but, afterwards, while my fellow students schmoozed and boozed, I felt detached from everything that was happening around me. Instead I stepped out onto the first-floor balcony overlooking Dean Street, getting soaked by the rain, questioning everything that was happening to me. I realized that I just didn't have 'it' in me any more: I felt as though I were flatlining. I had lost all my passion and enjoyment in life.

Nevertheless, somehow I managed to graduate. But I was still at a complete loss as to what to do next. I returned to London.

11

IBD

Can't get no relief, can't get no sleep.
The only thing left, the next dreaded heartbeat.

Jonny Benjamin, untitled poem

WHEN I RETURNED HOME after graduating, I started working as a childminder, a job I loved. In addition, my sister-in-law's father, a wedding photographer, gave me a job as his assistant. I was not well enough to keep down a regular full-time job, but I realized how fortunate I was to have all these supportive people around me who wanted to see me get better. I loved looking after children – they are refreshingly non-judgmental and open-minded – but secretly I was experiencing crippling anxiety. This was made worse by the abdominal pain and constant discomfort I had started to suffer. I kept picking up bugs from the children, and I felt as though I were constantly suffering from gastric flu.

I had experienced gastric flu a few times before, but my stomach never seemed to go back to normal after my first bout that year. And it had never been as bad as this before. The cramps were excruciating, I was constantly fatigued, utterly exhausted, and had blood in my stools. I became convinced I was dying; I have always had a tendency to panic. In fact I would say that I'm a hypochondriac, the sort of person who reads up his symptoms on the internet and ends up believing he has every single disease mentioned. So was I just overreacting?

After several fruitless visits to my GP, I was finally referred to a gastroenterologist for tests. A whole battery of invasive, undignified tests, in fact, including a colonoscopy and an endoscopy, as well as blood tests. I watched the colonoscopy on the screen as it happened, and despite my discomfort I was compelled by the science and technology behind it. I realized just how amazing the human body is, and how much I'd always taken it for granted.

The doctors discovered an inflammation in my large bowel, and after a later MRI scan, during which my intestines were examined in more detail, I was diagnosed with Crohn's, a debilitating and chronic inflammatory bowel disease, which is treatable but not curable. To say that I was upset would be an understatement: first to be diagnosed with schizoaffective disorder, and now this? But I was in so much abdominal pain I just wanted it resolved.

Initially, I was prescribed Mesalazine, an anti-inflammatory, but it didn't work, so my consultant put me on Prednisolone, a steroid which had a disastrous effect on my mental health. Almost immediately I developed extreme mood swings and became increasingly paranoid and suicidal – all in the course of a single week. Day by day I became more unstable and paranoid, and less and less able to function. There was one day in particular when I decided to clean my room and my obsessive-compulsive tendencies escalated to the point where I kept repositioning objects again and again. The whole process took me twelve hours.

Still embarrassed by my diagnosis, I hadn't disclosed my mental-health history to my consultant. As it transpired, if you are prone to psychosis, Prednisolone can trigger an episode.

After about a week of mounting obsessive thoughts and paranoia, I became suicidal once again. One evening, when my parents were out, I started to cry uncontrollably, unable to stop. Eventually I managed to call a friend who came around immediately. Even with him there, I behaved maniacally, one minute crying hysterically, the next laughing. I felt that I was right back where I had been before being admitted to hospital: out of control.

When my parents came home, I had to admit that I had stopped seeing my psychiatrist. They begged me to go back, and to come off the Prednisolone. I did, but even for a few days afterwards I was unable to leave the house, and when I finally ventured out to Camden Market – admittedly not the wisest choice considering how crowded it gets – I was overcome by sheer terror. My heart was racing and I couldn't breathe. I felt as though I were suffocating.

The consultant decided that it would be best to do another colonoscopy. I'll never forget it: the specialist was running late on the day of the test and rushed it from the get-go. He pushed the camera in so quickly that it twisted inside my colon, causing me the worst pain ever. At some point, no doubt panicking, three nurses had to sit on top of me in an attempt to push down my bulging abdomen, as I writhed in agony.

To add insult to injury, after the ordeal was finally over, they posted the wrong test results to me. To my horror, these results showed a severely diseased colon, one that – even to the untrained eye – looked as though it was in an advanced state of disintegration. Then I noticed the birthday in the corner of the image: from the 1930s. It was a mix-up.

When I finally received my new diagnosis, Irritable Bowel Syndrome, I was relieved. The whole episode had been pretty awful, but at least IBS was a less severe condition than Crohn's. I was prescribed Mesalazine once again, but my symptoms persisted. After my last few experiences I was becoming more wary of conventional medicine and instead I looked into alternative treatments. I learned about pre- and probiotics, which aid digestion, and used those along with aloe vera capsules. While they by no means cured me, they did alleviate some of the symptoms. To this day I believe that there is a strong correlation between anxiety and inflammatory bowel disease (which covers a number of conditions), and this has strengthened my resolve to stay as healthy as possible, both mentally and physically.

This latest diagnosis had a huge psychological effect on me: once again, it was a big knock, and once again there seemed to be a general lack of understanding, support or even information. Needless to say, that one week on steroids didn't help. When I went to Camden Market after my steroid-induced psychosis, I felt everyone was watching me, especially the security guards, who I was convinced suspected me of stealing. In fact, that episode has had a long-term effect on me; to this day I often feel watched by surveillance cameras, and extremely self-conscious and uncomfortable when I spot a security guard in a shop. I become convinced that they are following me down the aisles.

That day in Camden, I didn't even end up buying what I had gone there for; I had to leave empty-handed after a short time walking around. And the journey home was no less excruciating; the Tube was a particularly difficult place for me to be. I couldn't sit on the seats that face each other, and had to opt for the ones at the end of the carriage, where you perch rather than sit; at least they face the direction of the aisle rather than your fellow passengers. On the bus, I always tried to sit at the front so I didn't need to worry about anyone turning around to look at me.

Having a physical condition on top of a mental one left me frustrated and angry and, just as in the aftermath of the schizophrenia diagnosis, these feelings were compounded by a sense of embarrassment. Without wanting to downplay its seriousness, something like diabetes would have at least been easier to talk about. With IBD, however, there was such an indignity surrounding the symptoms and the procedures, it seemed almost too much to bear. Now, on top of the stigma of mental illness, there was the stigma of a thoroughly unglamorous physical condition. And just as with schizoaffective disorder, IBD tends to strike at a time when we are arguably at our most vulnerable: in our twenties, just as our peers forge careers or further their education, or party like there's no tomorrow and embark on relationships. I desperately wanted to fit in, but I felt like an outsider. I desperately wanted to talk to my friends about it all, but found it too embarrassing. It felt as though my body was falling apart, and there seemed little I could do about it. Just to make matters worse, I also suddenly developed severe dandruff.

Everything was happening at once, but I felt unable to articulate my feelings at the time, so much so that I even stopped writing my diary. I no longer had the words to express my intense feelings of anger, embarrassment and frustration. I bottled them all up instead, to the point where I began to grind my teeth at night until my gums hurt.

In the absence of any offers of psychological support from the doctors, I joined Crohn's & Colitis UK, Britain's leading IBD charity. This helped, especially reading about other people's stories in their magazine. I was also surprised to learn that Crohn's disease and ulcerative colitis are far more prevalent in the Jewish than in the non-Jewish community; in fact, Ashkenazi Jews are four times more likely to develop one of these conditions and, according to one study quoted in *Doctor's Digest*, 'in Stamford Hill in the UK, for example, amongst individuals 20 years or older, the prevalence of Crohn's disease and ulcerative colitis is approximately 20 in 1,000 of the Jewish population as compared with 5 in 1,000 of the local non-Jewish population.' Yet we had never been taught anything about IBD in school.

During this time of great mental and physical pain, it became more important than ever for me to try to achieve and maintain some peace of mind. There was one book in particular which, along with the IBD organization, helped me through that difficult period: *Mindfulness: Finding Peace in a Frantic World* by Mark Williams and Danny Penman. In what would become something of a pattern, mindfulness saw me through an extremely challenging period in my life.

Physically, things have never gone back to how they were before the diagnosis, when my digestive health was relatively good. I've tried various diets over the years, including Paleo, which is based on what our ancestors ate, i.e. grass-fed meats, eggs, fish, vegetables, and seeds, and no sugar or grains. I managed to stay on it for several months, and it did make a difference by resetting my digestive system, but it was very difficult to stick to. Cutting out sugar, including fruit, was particularly difficult, and shopping became a complicated task. So many supermarket foods contain these 'forbidden' ingredients. At one point, my doctor suspected I might be lactose-intolerant, but as my local NHS trust had cut services for testing food allergies, his advice was simply to cut out lactose. No definitive answer or treatment plan, only a perfunctory, 'We've done the best we can. Off you go.' Frustrated, I once again turned to alternative remedies, but after spending a fortune to little avail, I lost patience. *Screw it. You get your hopes up and when it doesn't work you're crushed. You might as well just give up.* I resigned myself to the fact that I would never be the same again.

Over the years, I have learned to avoid certain foods (you don't want to be near me after I've had a pizza), and still need to be careful what and when I eat, especially in social situations or while at work. Initially, the doctors told me to have more fibre, but this actually made my symptoms worse; I have since learned that not everybody needs more fibre in their diet. In fact, the whole experience has been a learning curve, and I now know, mostly through trial and error, what my triggers are: alcohol, spicy foods, too much bread and dairy.

In 2016 my symptoms suddenly worsened and this time the specialists opted to give me a sigmoidoscopy. This test is far less invasive than a colonoscopy, as it uses a shorter, flexible tube – a welcome relief after my previous experience. And now I was given yet another diagnosis: ulcerative colitis. Although similar to Crohn's disease (which is why the two are often confused, and can be difficult to diagnose), it is generally less severe as it only affects the large bowel and tends to lead to fewer complications. This time I was prescribed anti-inflammatory suppositories, and I did fairly well for a while, but it was all another reminder that, as it is with my mental health, my battle with IBD is ongoing.

As is the stigma attached to it. Not only is IBD not talked about in society, in my experience, but it strikes me that people are far more likely to tell someone about a broken bone than Crohn's, colitis, depression or schizophrenia. We simply don't talk enough about our digestive systems *or* our brains, and yet they are closely linked.

On a lighter note, once when I confided in my doctor about the embarrassment of suffering from wind, he suggested 'flatulence pants'. I thought he was joking, but they do in fact exist. Based on technology commonly applied to chemical warfare suits, they feature an activated carbon lining that is designed to absorb any offending odours, according to the leading brand's online ads. Well, at least I wasn't having to wear those just yet.

12

Letters to Amy

from Survival of the Fearless

Monday's fear is mild,
Tuesday's fear takes hold,
By Wednesday I am crumbling,
And the doubt takes its toll.

Jonny Benjamin, *Pill After Pill*

IT WAS JUNE 2011 and I'd been home from university for two years, doing my odd jobs and trying to manage my symptoms. I'd also started to make YouTube videos with a view to helping other people understand my schizoaffective disorder. One of my great sources of joy and constant delight throughout this time was the music of Amy Winehouse. Amy's lyrics made me feel less lonely. She helped keep me going. I decided to write her a letter.

Dear Amy,

I've never written a fan letter before and I'm not so great at articulating what I want to say, but I've been meaning to write to you for so long just to say thank you, Amy.

Briefly, my name is Jonny and I'm 24. I live in northwest London. I know it's a cliché and I'm sure you've heard it before, but the moment I first heard your music literally changed my life. It was October 2006 and a girlfriend had dragged me shopping to Manchester's Trafford Centre and I was standing in New Look when 'Rehab' started playing. I was rooted to the spot by your voice, the beat, the words you were singing. It was almost as if you were singing the story of my life at that moment. I was in my second year studying drama at Manchester School of Theatre and going through a pretty major breakdown.

My friend left to go on to the next shop, but I said I had to stay right there until the song had finished. As soon as I got home, I Googled the song's lyrics, downloaded it and played it on loop. It was something I could finally relate to.

The lines about drinking particularly resonated. I'd started drinking heavily as a way out of depression. I'd been depressed since I was 16 and tried various medications but the hole I was in was just getting deeper. I also had schizophrenia but it hadn't been diagnosed yet.

I was struggling to accept my sexuality at the time as well. Coming from a Jewish family, I was constantly faced with 'When are you going to find a nice Jewish girl? When are you going to get married?' etc. – you know how it is. All the pressure was overwhelming to say the least, but I always told myself that at the end of the day, no matter how deep the shit I was in, I could go home and listen to you, Nina, Aretha and Etta, and everything would be ok.

As soon as I heard your voice begin to sing, Amy, at once all the pain, fear and particularly the loneliness, seemed to fade away.

On the day of its release I bought *Back to Black* and it's lived in my car's CD player ever since! Intermittently with *Frank* of course! Although I'd never really been in love, I'd felt enough loss in my life to relate. I was increasingly isolating myself and spending time in my car to avoid seeing anyone. Looking back, I don't know how I would have coped without your music there. I truly mean that. There was nothing else that could communicate my thoughts and feelings.

On 25 July 2007 I went to see you at the ICA. You blew my mind that night, Amy. I am constantly listening to the live recording that iTunes released of that gig. Me and my friend Sarah were standing front row by your backing singers and she was convinced Zalon was eyeing her up all night. She asked for a photo with him after the show and spent ages chatting to him, whilst one of your crew handed me the set list that was stuck to the floor of the stage. I think we were both as euphoric as each other!

The next few months were pretty tough, as I know they were for you. In December 2007 I was admitted to hospital. 'Love Is a Losing Game' had just been released and I remember playing it non-stop in the days leading up to me being admitted. I'd just had my first sexual relationship with a guy and it was over so suddenly, without explanation. I think that tipped me over the edge and I was ready to quit life.

I was diagnosed with schizoaffective disorder and stayed in hospital for six weeks. The worst part about it was that I wasn't allowed music for the first few weeks because I was on suicide watch. They were concerned I might strangle myself with my earphones, so I was only allowed to use them when someone was present, watching me. But that didn't feel right. To me, listening to music is such a personal experience sometimes, sort of like prayer or meditation. I'd lost belief in my faith, and music was the only thing that ever remained constant.

Everything changed the day this happened. Now I feel labelled for life. People changed towards me. If I go quiet in a crowd, or want some time to myself, people are concerned that I'm having a relapse or something. I know it's only because they care, but sometimes the stigma that comes with mental illness or addiction is harder than actually having to deal with the problem itself.

I have had a few relapses since I was discharged in January 2008. I developed and recovered from an eating disorder, and now anxiety is now my biggest hurdle but I'll get through it. There's so much I want to achieve in life.

I want the old Jonny back. I feel like a shadow of the person I was before my breakdown. I was doing well at drama school and they said I had a lot of potential. I was never confident, but I could go on stage, into the spotlight, and here I was happiest. Now my passion, well, it's there but I just can't seem to unlock it. I can barely hold eye contact with someone nowadays or make a conversation, let alone go on stage. Seeing you looking so healthy and radiant recently, and reading about your performance at the 100 Club fills me with more strength to overcome my struggles than any amount of medication or therapy has ever given me.

If you're anything like me then it's hard to accept praise. I didn't want to write you a gushing letter about how talented and special you are because sometimes your demons stand firmly in the way of self-belief, and you could be told a million times how wonderful you are, but at the end of the day it's that one negative comment that you hold on to. Instead I'd rather let you know how much of an impact your music has had on my life.

I don't want you thinking I'm a stalker or anything but I carry your picture around with me on a key ring my friends gave me when I was in hospital. It's my favourite picture of you in a beautiful orange strapless dress. Everyone knows how much I adore you and I must have been bought your 'I Told You I Was Trouble: Live from London' DVD at least half a dozen times from different friends and family. My mum's always saving the articles she spots of you in the *Jewish Chronicle*!

All I have to do is look at that key ring, close my eyes and I'm back at the ICA. I've attached some photos of that night with this letter. It is one of the happiest moments of my life, along with my niece being born a year ago. I've already got her first CD lined up that I'm going to play to her. Can you guess what it is?

I hope people aren't putting too much pressure on you about releasing the new album. Do it whenever you feel ready, Amy. Your true fans are the ones that will wait. We're right beside you all the way. And if you ever lack the self-belief you need to perform or a voice in your mind says you're not good enough, please remember that there is <u>always</u> someone out there believing in you, Amy, at that particular moment, and not just me but countless others! 'To touch one life' is to touch many and you've certainly touched mine.

Best of luck for your upcoming dates in Europe. I know you'll do great. I don't know if I've written all I set out to say before writing this letter. I really just wanted to express my gratitude toward you and your music. I hope I haven't overstepped the mark at all. I know you've been through a lot of shit and I won't pretend to know what it's been like. I just hope you can take something away from this fan whom you have given so much to. You have also inspired me to write poetry and songs, some of which are on YouTube, and where I've also created a project about trying to end the stigma attached to mental illness entitled 'I'm Just Human'. My YouTube channel is www.youtube.com/johnjusthuman

With much love,

Jonny

A month later, I was shocked to hear the news: Amy Winehouse had been found dead in her Camden flat. I was devastated, and it sent me spiralling downwards.

Before Amy Winehouse passed away that summer, I'd felt like our lives were mirroring each other's. When she went through her really bad spell, I went to hospital. When she was on the up, so was I. I was working at a wedding when I got the news. 'I'm not surprised,' was the comment I kept hearing, but I'd been convinced that she'd conquered her demons. She was my hero, and heroes don't die. The next day I went to lay flowers outside her home. There were the press. Front-row position. They'd torn her apart, and now they had come one last time, suddenly realizing her talent and recognizing their loss.

My physical condition made things so much worse during this period. Now, on top of the endless pain and discomfort, there was grief for Amy, too. As isolation set in, I decided to devote myself to making a tribute video to Amy for YouTube.

Two months later, it was Yom Kippur. Instead of going to synagogue and fasting, I stayed at home and ate. Even when my mum and dad went to my brother and sister-in-law's to break the fast I stayed at home. *Bad Jew I am.* I felt that my whole existence was pointless. My documentary about Amy had gone down like a lead balloon. And of course I was still troubled by my inflammatory bowel disease: endless spasms in my stomach, not to mention the constant gas and burping that came with it. I wasn't absorbing anything but going to the toilet all the time and thus losing weight. And I was tired all the time.

By now I despised myself so much that I couldn't even look at myself without blushing. For two years I'd tried to do so many things, written so many letters, and what had I got out of it? Nothing. I was bitter. Disappointed. But still convinced I had some talent, I was desperate to be famous. I wasn't alone – this was when *The X Factor* was at the peak of its popularity. Everybody seemed to want their five minutes of fame and fortune.

My thinking around this time was very muddled. Despite seeing what had happened to Amy Winehouse, being well known still seemed like the solution to life's problems. Living in London, I felt trampled on as soon as I left the front door. By the time I'd made my way onto the Tube and got off at my destination I just wanted to curl up into a ball and be done with the nightmare that was living in this city. I was reduced to a shadow and couldn't speak a sentence without stumbling over my words. Yet still I wanted that damn fame. I wasn't interested in the fortune. I only wanted fame in order to help others and change people's thinking.

This world was screwed. The economy was in tatters and getting worse. The same went for society: the riots in London that August had been utterly shocking but sadly not completely unsurprising. So much tension and despair. I wanted to be a hero. I'd always wanted to be loved and I needed acceptance.

What could I do, in a world where I felt like I was the only person around who seemed to give a damn? About others, about the state of things. I had no answers, but I tried to console myself:

You'll be ok, J. Perhaps I'll never find fame or love. But they don't equate to happiness. And that's really what I need now. Not every day, but a bit more joy and particularly freedom is essential. And so it's time. You might not have the things you want out of life, J, but you have something unique and that is you. No one else has that. It's a gift.

13

Media

Insanity – a perfectly rational adjustment to an insane world.

R. D. Laing

IN EARLY 2012, I decided to go back to Manchester. Luckily, I was able to stay with friends from university and, after seeing some of my YouTube video logs, or vlogs, I'd landed my first job with Nine Lives Media, who were producing a documentary for a series on mental health called 'It's a Mad World', commissioned by BBC Three. The production company wanted me to present it and also do research for the programme.

Getting my first full-time job was a bittersweet experience. On the one hand, it gave me a purpose and more confidence, and I enjoyed going to work every morning. On the other, I was still wrapped up in anxiety, not helped by the fact that our office was open plan. I had always hated speaking on the phone, especially to strangers because I couldn't read their facial expressions or body language, and knowing that I was being overheard by my colleagues made this ten times worse. I remember a call to the mental-health charity SANE, when the person at the other end asked me questions and I found that I couldn't speak. I choked on my words, unable to breathe. From then on I pretended to make phone calls from the office and even left fake voice messages, while secretly sneaking out and phoning people from outside the building. At around this time I decided to try beta-blockers again to combat my anxiety. Unfortunately, they interrupted my sleep even further. And yet I was so hard on myself at this time: I wanted to be like my friends who by now had been working for years. I was desperate to 'function' like them, to be more 'productive', but instead I felt guilty and inadequate. The only thing that kept me going was my passion for this documentary we were working on.

However, the more research I conducted, the more shocked I became by what was going on in the mental-health system, in particular with regards to young people. I'd had some idea how CAMHS, the Child and Adolescent Mental Health Services, operated, but I didn't realize the extent to which young people were falling through the net when their support was stopped at the age of eighteen, and they were left either to fend for themselves, or put on a long waiting list for adult mental-health services. It became very clear that NICE (the National Institute for Care and Health Excellence) guidelines were not always followed regarding the transition from CAMHS to adult services. I was shocked to discover how adversely young people's mental health could be affected by this – even, in some cases, leading to suicide.

As I have said earlier, at this time I was suffering from very low self-esteem and severe paranoia, always worrying what other people thought of me. This wasn't helped by my impaired ability to read people's facial expressions. My assumption that they all disliked me had been shaped by one particular experience at the age of nineteen when I'd talked to a stranger at a birthday party. After we had been chatting for about half an hour, her friend joined in the conversation, only for the first stranger to turn to her and say, 'Don't talk to him, he's really boring.' From then on, every time I was in a social situation, I would hear this voice, especially if the other person appeared to be distracted, was looking at their phone, or avoided eye contact. The stranger's voice, and her words, haunted me for years.

Meanwhile, I was shaking a lot and had become prone to extreme blushing, which in a vicious cycle caused me even more social anxiety, made me extremely self-conscious and led to terrible mood swings. Then, at a charity event in Manchester, I was offered free CBT, Cognitive Behavioural Therapy, and this time it was a revelation.

Although I'd tried it in the past, I hadn't got much out of it. This time, however, CBT really helped me change my thinking patterns. It helped stop the spiral of thoughts telling me that I wasn't good enough: not good enough for the work I was doing, not good enough to deserve a relationship. With the help of talking therapy and set exercises, including putting myself into situations I normally avoided – such as going on dates – I gradually began to think differently, and to rationalize my fears.

It wasn't easy. Creating a new pathway in the brain takes a lot of work.

Around the same time, I also went on a mindfulness course in Devon, paid for by the company I worked for. Even though my employers still didn't know the full extent of my anxiety, they had seen my YouTube vlogs about mental health, and were very supportive. When mindfulness had first been suggested to me in hospital, years earlier, I'd felt strongly that it wouldn't be for me. I'd imagined people sitting around cross-legged, looking spaced-out and chanting. A therapist had given me a CD by Jon Kabat-Zinn, the founder of MBSR (Mindfulness-Based Stress Reduction), but over the next few years it just gathered dust on my shelf.

So it was with some trepidation that I went off to the retreat. Sharpham Estate in Totnes, Devon, is an impressive eighteenth-century Palladian villa overlooking the River Dart and surrounded by lush countryside. Despite the beautiful setting, I was still anxious, and doubted that I would be able to take part in any of the sessions. I had so much nervous energy, how would I even manage to sit still for long enough? Would I be thrown off the course?

Over the next five days, I took part in group sessions with about nine other people, guided by the excellent mindfulness coaches, Sarah and Duncan. We practised meditation, creative writing and even canoeing. For the first time, I learned about self-acceptance, self-forgiveness and self-compassion – concepts I had always assumed were reserved for other people, and not for me. On 31 August 2012, I wrote:

> How can one mind hold so much unkindness for itself, yet place such unconditional love upon everyone else?

The course proved to be a pivotal moment in my life: at last I had managed to achieve some peace of mind. In fact, it was such a revelation that on my return I finally listened to Jon Kabat-Zinn's *Mindfulness for Beginners* CD. To this day, I remember how I felt after the first ten-minute meditation, how attuned I was to the sound, sight and sensation of simply washing my hands. I was wholly in the present, everything seemed clear and still, and all my worries and fears had vanished. Peace of mind.

At Sharpham, I also realized how important creative writing was to me. I wrote this poem, 'Evergreen', there:

> When she no longer feels her heartbeat,
> She flies to pastures green,
> And there she rests her aching mind,
> Beneath the shade of the Evergreen.

Peace swims through her veins,
No harm can touch her here;
No dread, no doubt, no demon,
To awaken her clenched in fear.

The breeze soothes over her skin,
Brings new life to weary eyes;
So tired of watching this world,
Falling by the wayside.

Finally, a smile,
Graces lips so often locked,
By senses soaked in numbness,
And a heart too long been stopped.

Now, here, it beats once again,
Deep within pastures green.
Her mind, still, but awoken
'Neath the shade of the Evergreen.

I tried hard to stay connected with my newfound mindfulness techniques, especially in 2013 when filming for the documentary finally started. We travelled around the country to talk to young people about the mental-health care they'd received – or hadn't received, as was sadly often the case. At the time, 2,000 psychiatric beds had been cut in England alone (these numbers have increased now) and although, according to the guidelines, patients at risk from self-harm or suicide should have been assessed both physically and psychologically, in 50 per cent of all cases this wasn't happening. Instead, patients were discharged without having been seen by a psychiatric nurse or psychiatrist. There simply weren't enough mental-health specialists in the hospitals, due to a lack of funding. Most of the young people I met had been released without a referral or any advice. As one of them, Emma, said to me, 'They make you feel like a burden.'

One of the most poignant parts of making the documentary was when I travelled to Belfast to meet a family whose son had taken his own life. Christopher had had to wait for more than eight hours in A&E and, even though he'd revealed to staff that he was planning to self-harm and he needed help, he was repeatedly told that someone would see him 'in half an hour'. But nobody did. Eventually, he gave up and went home. His mental state became increasingly worse over the next four days, and on the fifth day his body was found in a Belfast Park. He was only nineteen. Standing by his graveside, his devastated mother said something terribly tragic: 'One of the hardest gifts to buy a child is a headstone. It's the final gift.'

Christopher Ferrin was just one of around 1,600 young people who take their lives every year in the UK, many of them while waiting for vital treatment. CBT, for example, has an average waiting time of at least six months. And, according to a study carried out around the time of Christopher's death, only 4 per cent of young people experienced a good transition from child to adult services. The results of my interviews and research left me incredibly frustrated and angry, but also made me feel inspired by all the young people who had overcome major obstacles, and shown remarkable strength and resilience. In many cases, they were proud of having 'done it' for themselves. As Emma pointed out: 'If I had waited on "them", I'd have been a goner.'

Another positive thing I took away from filming the documentary was the sheer number of initiatives starting to crop up. One of these was a mindfulness class designed especially for young people.

I attended one of these in the Lake District with a few of the young people I had interviewed. And I took heart at seeing the development of apps such as Doc Ready, which helps young people struggling with their mental health to prepare for their first visit to the doctor, so they can express themselves clearly and ask for the right kind of help. Speaking to these teenagers, and to Christopher's family in Belfast in particular, made me even more determined to focus my life on campaigning for better mental health for all.

Unfortunately, not long after we had finished filming, the BBC decided to change the shape of the documentary and rename it 'Failed by the NHS'. I was opposed to this: although it was vital to highlight NHS shortcomings and call for more funding, there were (and still are) amazing people working within the system, often under very difficult circumstances. More importantly, however, I didn't want to discourage people with mental-health problems from seeking help.

By the time the documentary aired, I felt like a pawn in somebody else's game. And, unsurprisingly, there was a backlash from viewers, who complained that the NHS deserved our support, not our criticism. The whole experience left me feeling angry with the BBC and disheartened with television. Nevertheless, I continued to work on other projects with Nine Lives Media, determined to find a way to get mental-health issues the media attention that they so desperately needed.

14

Love Affairs

Loneliness

I tell myself I don't need no one,
but when the day is done,
and home I've come,
loneliness leaves me numb.

Jonny Benjamin, unpublished poem

ONE NIGHT IN MANCHESTER my friend Phil took me to a club on Canal Street and introduced me to a fellow student, Duncan (not his real name), who was studying nursing. We hit it off straight away, and I was instantly attracted to him: roughly around my age, he had a friendly face, strikingly blue eyes, short dark hair, and a ginger tinge to his beard. He was also charming and funny and had a thick Glaswegian accent; I was very drawn to him. After Phil left, I desperately wanted to kiss Duncan, but he was keen to go somewhere else, somewhere more private and romantic – instantly another point in his favour.

Everything was great at first – exciting and new. Finally, I was in love with someone and the feeling lasted for several months. But I was still suffering from anxiety. One day, as we were walking back to Duncan's flat, I bumped into some old friends and suddenly had a panic attack. Feeling self-conscious, I struggled to talk to my friends, but started to shake and felt as though I couldn't breathe. Although Duncan was aware of my condition, he laughed it off: 'You're so silly.'

Looking back, this incident was the beginning of the end. I began to realize that Duncan could sometimes be quite unkind and even cruel; never openly aggressive, but nasty in a snide and undermining way: he always knew how to get to me. To make matters worse, he was not at all supportive when I found it difficult to go out and socialize – something that struck me as odd considering that he was training to be a nurse. Surely he should be more compassionate?

Yet for a while I still saw a future with him. This was my first long-term relationship, and despite everything I was in love and wanted to work things out. Unfortunately, Duncan didn't see it that way. We continued to see each other for a few months, but as he grew colder and more distant towards me, I realized that it wasn't going to last.

One day at his flat, I decided to ask him what was going on. Duncan shrugged. 'I'm really busy with my course. I think we should leave this for a few months. But if I meet someone in the meantime . . .'

This was the moment when, for the first time, my heart was truly broken. I can still remember the drive home. It was a Friday evening, rush hour, and I was stuck in traffic, bawling my eyes out, aware that the people in the cars next to me could see me. It took me quite a while to get over Duncan, and six months on I was clearly still grieving.

Fuck you at the bar, I know you've seen me and you broke my heart. Long ago when we first met, no amount of spirits could let me forget. And now I hate you with every bone in my body, for you're in love with him and I'm left with nobody. So

I stand here and my soul it breaks; whilst every inch of him is
yours to take.

A few months later, along came David (not his real name) and I
embarked on my second serious relationship. He chased me for a
while on Facebook as we had friends in common, and we arranged
to meet for our first date in a bar in Didsbury on a Saturday afternoon. When I walked in, David was already waiting for me and
Carole King's 'I Feel the Earth Move' was playing. I was attracted
to David as soon as I saw him. He was of Middle Eastern heritage,
and he was gorgeous. I thought: *This is the moment everyone talks
about when they meet The One.*

We went on to a tapas bar and got drunk on sangria. And that
was it; I fell in love with him there and then. Afterwards we went
back to his flat and I stayed the night, convinced that the Carole
King song had been a sign.

One day, fairly soon after we first met, we were on the couch
at David's flat, getting it on, when his ex suddenly walked in
to collect his stuff. I'd only just found out that they had separated quite recently. The whole situation was so embarrassing that
I almost can't bear to remember it. In hindsight, I should have
known that David was on the rebound, but things were going really
well (much better than with Duncan) and I felt even more deeply
in love.

My anxiety continued to be an issue, however, and to make
matters worse my IBS started to flare up. Overall, David dealt
with the anxiety better than Duncan, but he found it difficult to
talk about my conditions. He started to get impatient and annoyed
when we were food shopping and I was worrying about what I
could and couldn't eat.

Then one night when we were in bed together, I suddenly lost my libido. I had no idea what was happening; I fancied David, so what was going on? I was so embarrassed that I became agitated and had a meltdown there and then, insisting that I needed to leave. David eventually managed to calm me down, but nothing was the same afterwards. The gap between us widened and he grew colder. As he began to text less and less, my anxiety grew more and more.

On a work trip to Edinburgh in 2013, I got extremely drunk one evening and decided to call David to ask for a straight answer to all the worries I had about our relationship. To my absolute horror, he confessed that he still had feelings for his ex and couldn't see a future for us. Madly in love and heartbroken, I was so distressed and overwhelmed by despair that I suddenly felt suicidal again. Thankfully, this time I asked for help. I called Maytree, a foundation in north London that offers those who are suicidal short-term accommodation and support. I told the lady on the phone that my anxiety and IBS were really bad, that I needed help. I cried for a long time that night but eventually the woman, who was extremely empathetic and patient, calmed me down.

Although I've met guys in the years since then, that was my last proper relationship. I've been desperate for a boyfriend since my mid-twenties, convinced that if somebody loves me unconditionally, it will save me. My fantasies revolve around meeting a journalist in New York; for some reason this is my ultimate dream scenario.

At times my quest has led me to extreme measures. On a trip to New York once, I ran up a phone bill of hundreds of pounds using dating apps. Back in London, I spent one Valentine's Day walking through Hampstead Heath, hoping to find somebody in the park, surrounded by couples holding hands. Another time I saw someone on the train and became convinced that we were destined to be together, so much so that I followed him to his work. Part of me knows that another person can't really complete me and that my struggles won't suddenly vanish if I find The One. Still, it's nice to dream.

15

Media Campaign

The worst loneliness is not to be comfortable with yourself.

Mark Twain

AFTER 'FAILED BY THE NHS' was broadcast in the summer of 2013, I was contacted by a film company in south London, Postcard Productions, who wanted to meet me. Around the same time, I had also attracted the attention of one of the leading mental-health charities, Rethink Mental Illness, who called with the wonderful news that I had won the first ever Janey Antoniou Award, named after the extraordinary campaigner who lost her life in a psychiatric hospital. Rethink Mental Illness had been founded in 1972 by relatives of people diagnosed with schizophrenia, who found that there was very little public support out there. In 2002 it adopted the name Rethink, which then expanded to become Rethink Mental Illness in 2011, though it remains registered as The National Schizophrenia Fellowship. And now they wanted me to become an ambassador for them! I was delighted.

I had a few meetings with Postcard in London. Both Postcard and Rethink Mental Illness had picked up on my story about the bridge and suggested that I try and find the stranger. I had thought about this myself, of course, but decided that it would be futile because my memory of that day was so fuzzy. But now that both Rethink Mental Illness and Postcard had proposed the idea for a documentary, I was in two minds: on the one hand, it would raise awareness of the issues I cared about; on the other, I was hesitant about going so public with my story. Added to this, my parents were understandably concerned about bringing up the past and how it would affect me.

What swayed me in the end was the platform it would give me to bring mental-health issues to the attention of the wider public. I had recently learned more about suicide, and was shocked to discover that it was the biggest killer of men under fifty. So I agreed, and Rethink Mental Illness and Postcard decided to launch their campaign on the sixth anniversary of that day on the bridge: 14 January 2014.

By this time I was already vlogging on YouTube and receiving more and more positive messages from viewers. This made going public with my story seem worthwhile. One of the messages was from a fourteen-year-old who had been struggling with their own mental-health issues, who told me, 'You don't know how much you have helped me.' Another said I'd changed his mind about taking his own life.

But my bubble was burst when for the first time I found myself being trolled. People accused me of being all sorts of things: 'a shit actor', a 'fake, attention-seeking prick', 'a drug addict who was hoping to get free prescription drugs if he pretended to be crazy'. One commented that I didn't behave like a 'schizofrenic [sic]' person, and another that I 'edited well for being mentally ill.' Receiving these vile, abusive messages brought back my reservations about making the documentary. Concerned, Postcard asked me whether I would be OK to continue. I summoned up my courage and insisted I'd be fine.

Finally the day of the launch arrived. We'd named the campaign #FindMike because I couldn't remember the name of the stranger. Rethink Mental Illness had booked an appearance for me on

Daybreak, ITV's breakfast show at the time, and I was due to be interviewed by Lorraine Kelly and Aled Jones. A car came to pick me up. This was my first time on live TV, and I was so nervous I was convinced I would be unable to speak. But I did it – I went on and told my story. And then everything exploded.

As soon as I had finished on *Daybreak*, I was whisked off to BBC radio on Great Portland Street. From then on it was interview after interview with a range of different media, and cameras following my every step because we were filming it all for the documentary. It was a whirlwind.

That same day, between interviews, I went to Waterloo Bridge to hand out flyers, to see whether anyone recognized the story, or indeed the stranger I was trying to find. This January day was very different from the one six years earlier: although just as cold, there was bright sunshine. The whole experience was surprisingly lovely: having seen me on TV, people were offering their support, and everyone was very kind and friendly. Many even opened up to me about their own mental-health issues, and one woman said, 'I'm glad you didn't do it.'

A range of interviews followed, for a diverse range of audiences, ranging from the *Sun* newspaper to BBC's Radio 4. The response was overwhelming; the #FindMike campaign went viral on social media and the hashtag was trending on Twitter. That evening I went home to my parents, exhausted and drained. My mum told me the phone hadn't stopped ringing: amongst others, old classmates who hadn't known about that day on the bridge and my illness were now getting in touch.

The next few days passed in a flurry of further interviews. There was more media coverage, including from CNN, and of course all the filming for the documentary. As the campaign gained momentum, it was followed by 319 million people around the globe, and I appeared on TV in the US, Canada, Australia and Germany. Even celebrities got involved in the search: Stephen Fry, Boy George and Kate Nash retweeted the original appeal, and then Deputy Prime Minister Nick Clegg sent me a message of support. And soon several leads started to come in, from people claiming they had been there, they had helped someone on the bridge that day. The majority seemed genuine, but inevitably there were a few attention seekers. We had a total of thirty-eight leads in all, each of them claiming they were 'Mike'.

For the first few days I was buzzing from all the interviews, but by the end of that week I came crashing down to reality. I looked at the photographs of all the potential 'Mikes' and didn't recognize a single one. All of a sudden, it dawned on me that we might never find him. Surely he must have seen at least some of the media coverage? Maybe he didn't want to be found? As time went on, a positive outcome seemed less and less likely. Would all the people involved in the campaign end up being terribly disappointed? The pressure was mounting.

Interest in the campaign began to trail off. During the second week, Rethink Mental Illness and Postcard both felt that we needed to wrap everything up, and even considered an alternative ending for the documentary. This was when I met Lisa, whose twin brother had killed himself by jumping off Tower Bridge. Although in the final cut of the documentary my interview with her is only a few minutes long, in reality we spoke for one and a half hours. To say that it was raw and emotional for both of us would be an understatement. Talking to this person, who had been close to someone who had killed himself, forced me to look at everything from the other side, and it was equally important for Lisa to hear my perspective. It was clearly consoling for her to learn that, in all likelihood, her brother would not have been in a state of mind where he could have considered the consequences of his actions for those closest to him. I told her that even as I was walking up to the bridge, I was praying for my mum and dad not to feel guilty, and I think this helped her. Yet listening to Lisa's story, I did feel guilty. It made me think about what it would have been like for my brother Elliot if I had, indeed, killed myself. And, even more than guilt, I felt an enormous amount of compassion and empathy with Lisa, and an overwhelming desire to help heal others.

It was an emotional but important interview and I wondered if maybe this could be the end of our documentary. Everyone involved in the campaign was convinced that 'Mike' would have come forward by now if he had wanted to be found.

Then, unbeknownst to me, Rethink Mental Illness received another lead – an email. It looked promising so they followed it up with an interview. And afterwards, they sat me down and said, 'Jonny, we think we've found him.'

16

The Stranger on the Bridge

Hi,

I hope this message gets through.

I was on the bridge that day and was the person to help Jonny.

I probably know that you may read this with some scepticism, however I assure that you that this email is 100 per cent genuine. I can recall the moment and details of our conversation on the bridge and the events with a lot of clarity and detail, even 6 years on.

I have emailed this rather than posted on Twitter or Facebook to avoid any unforeseen complications in establishing who helped Jonny.

My name is Neil Laybourn, I have worked in Covent Garden since 2007, travelling over Waterloo Bridge to work most mornings.

I would be delighted to help confirm all this and would love the opportunity to make contact with Jonny to reciprocate his genuine gratefulness to something I was fortunate to be able to be there for.

Please feel free to contact me in confidence.

Kindest regards,

Neil Laybourn

MY FIRST MEETING WITH 'Mike' was scheduled for late January 2014, a few days before my twenty-seventh birthday. I could hardly believe that it was finally going to happen. Waking up that morning, I was as nervous as on the day of the campaign launch. Would I recognize him? Would my nerves come across in the documentary? That would be so embarrassing! And what would I do when I saw him? Even though I'm not a touchy-feely person, I thought I'd hug him. Or maybe just go for a handshake. Definitely a handshake.

The meeting was arranged to take place in a room above a pub in Vauxhall, south London. It was, of course, vital for the production team to catch the very first moment we saw each other, and so I had instructions to wait upstairs while 'Mike' was on the ground floor. As fate would have it, we both needed the toilet at the same time, and it turned into a military operation to keep us apart.

Finally, I sat on the sofa in the upstairs room, ready to meet the stranger. Keen to make it look as natural as possible, the camera crew had advised him just to walk in and sit down next to me. And there he was, this tall, muscular young man with strawberry-blond hair. He had the biggest smile on his face . . . but me? I didn't recognize him at all. Nothing came to me.

Even when he hugged me, I was still unsure. He said, 'Fantastic to see you. I've seen you on TV. Seems like only good things have happened to you.'

There was something familiar about him, but I was confused, a bundle of nerves. I could only ask him over and over again whether he was OK.

'I'm fine, I'm fine,' he said.

It was only when we sat down and he made a distinctive gesture while talking, reaching out his hand to emphasize something, that everything from that day on the bridge suddenly came flooding back. It was an incredibly surreal and emotional experience. My face in my hands, all I could say was:

'Thank you so much. Wow. Before, it was all just a hazy memory, but now it's all coming back, you standing to one side of me.'

The man, who I was now told was called Neil, asked me whether I remembered how cold it had been: 'I saw you sitting there on the bridge, and I knew straightaway. You came into my vision and I knew what was happening. I didn't see how I could get to you, because there was quite a distance between us, you know? I kept walking, walking, walking.'

He said he then went up to me. 'Do you want me to tell you what happened?'

I nodded.

'I asked you, "Why are you sitting on the bridge?" and you told me you were going to take your life. I thought, "There's no way I'm going to let this guy jump."'

I realized that Neil didn't know much about my background, and so I ended up doing a lot of the talking after that, but he did tell me that he had been on his way to the Strand that morning, where he worked as a fitness trainer. As we continued talking, he stayed acutely attentive, gently inquisitive and friendly. There was a great warmth about him.

Annoyingly, halfway through our conversation, a lorry began reversing loudly outside and the camera crew became a little nervous about the sound quality. An ill-timed and yet strangely poignant reminder that everyday life was still going on all around us.

We talked for about ninety minutes, both forgetting about the cameras as I told Neil in great depth about my mental health. I said that he'd restored my faith in humanity that day. Just the fact that he'd taken the trouble to stop and talk to me.

'It's nice to know that I somehow made a difference. It must have been awful for you, mate,' Neil replied.

'It was you saying to me, "You can get through this", that there was another way. Thank you.'

Neil smiled. 'I'm proud of you.'

'It's strange. It feels like we're friends.'

'I have a feeling we will be now.'

When the cameras stopped rolling, Neil and I exchanged contact details. The team got champagne and we all celebrated our success. Later I would write in my diary that it was 'the greatest day of my life.'

17

The Comedown

It goes to my head. I need to come back to earth, and fast.

Diary entry, 9 March 2014

MY REUNION WITH NEIL and the media coverage that followed were such a high for me. Once it was announced that 'Mike' had been found, there was a huge flurry of activity on social media, and although Neil had never been in front of the cameras before, he proved to be a natural. It felt like the best present ever.

While the documentary was being edited, there were still bits and pieces about the campaign and the reunion in the media, and now I was being approached about potential book deals. Unbelievably, there was even interest in my life story from Paramount Pictures. However, I felt very ambiguous about all this: yes, it was great on some level, but I didn't know whether I was in the right place to sit down and write my autobiography. More than anything, I wanted to make a film about mental health around the world. I felt strongly that the time was right for me to do this. I was still young, and there was so much more I still wanted to achieve.

Inevitably, perhaps, I started to become so anxious about all this, so much so that I couldn't socialize with friends or even go into the open-plan Rethink Mental Illness offices where I was working. And whilst my paranoia was increasing, so was my ambition, to the point of self-delusion. February was hard: after suddenly being thrust into the spotlight, I fell out of it just as quickly. I was supposed to be happier than ever; that had been the plan. Instead I stopped looking after myself and became completely caught up in my own thoughts again.

Since starting work on the campaign, my delusions had come back with a vengeance. I was hearing the voice more frequently and finding communicating with others increasingly difficult. I'd thought I could change the world, but I was finding it hard enough to live in my own inner world – full of its habitual self-loathing. I was also having obsessive thoughts, especially about men: although I was starting to realize how hypercritical I was towards myself and how I needed to forgive myself and show myself some compassion, I still felt that I needed to find myself a man to gain confidence.

It was particularly hard dealing with the difficulty I had communicating with others – the blushing, blinking, and smiling. And it all seemed so silly when I wrote it down in my diary. What was even sillier was that I would show every other person on the planet some compassion bar myself. I never gave myself time any more. I mean, myself as I was, not the person I wanted to be. The person I wanted to be was the Jonny during the #FindMike campaign: the person who was 'famous'; a 'celebrity', as people had started calling me after the media attention.

On a Sunday in early March, three friends and I were driving back to London from Manchester after an engagement party. We were chatting to each other when one of them, who was sitting next to me in the back of the car, whispered, 'I can tell when you're being fake,' clearly referring to my conversation with the two people in the front:

It was like a blade through my self-esteem. Since that day
I've clung onto his words. Now I worry every time I speak to
someone that I'm coming across as fake. How sad is that? One
throwaway comment, and my existence becomes a struggle as
a result.

Much of my paranoia and anxiety over the next few months
stemmed from this incident. Intrusive, obsessive thoughts kept
telling me that I was 'fake'. As a result, I started to avoid people
and even stopped talking to friends on the phone. Once again, the
cyclical nature of my illness was becoming evident. But at least
now I had some tried-and-tested tools to help me regain my peace
of mind. I decided that I needed to get away from everything for a
while.

In April I travelled to a mindfulness retreat in Wales, held at
the Trigonos centre, a stunning estate situated on a lake in Snow-
donia, surrounded by meadows and woodlands. It was so good
to get away from the hustle and bustle of London! But I was still
unsettled. Over the first few days, according to my diary, I became
obsessed with 'Going Back' by Dusty Springfield, a song about lost
innocence and freedom.

It was no coincidence that I was obsessed with Dusty Springfield's song. Like many people who struggle with mental-health
issues, especially depression, I longed for what I perceived as child-
hood innocence, that curiosity and sense of wonder every time you
discover something new, even something as simple as a beautiful
flower or a snowflake. And now I was learning that through mindfulness it was possible to recapture that very essence of pure joy,
hope and peace of mind. In fact, you could argue that children
practise mindfulness naturally when they are enchanted by the
vitality of the moment, when everything seems possible.

I told the people at Trigonos that I had a form of schizophrenia. I felt that the world needed to know. Why? Because I was sure I could change the world. That was my vision: for the world to see me, an ordinary young man living with this disease. The attention would be good; it would help others who suffered. And yet maybe the reasoning behind it was not so good – was this just another delusion? That everyone would like me if I admitted to frailty? After all, weren't we all frail as human beings?

'Ay, there's the rub,' as Hamlet said.

For being liked by all human beings is impossible. What can we do, we who suffer so with tormented minds? My thoughts overflowed like one of the waterfalls we'd seen on a walk: cascading, colliding, and yet constant.

> I felt such peace today, such peace of mind.
>
> I must go, the heavens are tipping it down, and the midges are all over me. But I lived today, I felt every breath in my body. That's the meaning of life.
>
> As I wrote that last word, there was stillness in the air, by this lake, surrounded by these mountains, and then a sudden breeze, like a message from G-d, like a deliverance.

And then:

> Don't deliver this message. You are not the Messiah.
> Am I?
>
> Strong gated heart of mine. Be strong, unstable mind.
> Freedom will deliver itself with patience, and time.

I would achieve these moments of serenity and then suddenly my thoughts would all crash at a particular moment, and it was intense and overwhelming. But at least I was becoming more familiar with this pattern now, and learning through mindfulness how to let it be: 'Learn to surf the waves,' as Jon Kabat-Zinn said. I often castigated myself for my wandering mind during meditation. But this wandering mind was precisely why Kabat-Zinn told us to come back, again, again and again, without judgement. I was trying.

> I really was free at some point today. Other times I was racked by concern about past, future, and even present. There is one person in the group who hates me. I slip into my mind, and it's troubled. And I'm self-critical, chronically so. Why? I don't need to judge. I just need to hold it in awareness. That's all.

Over time, I did find lasting peace of mind at the retreat, thanks both to the beautiful setting and the quality of the course. The instructors were compassionate and grounded, and really connected with us. I remember one young man in particular who was grieving after losing his mum. His pain really affected me, and I've often wondered what has become of him. Within days of arriving back in London, however, that fragile sense of peace was slipping away again.

Then one Friday afternoon that spring I received an email from a TV company in Texas. They wanted to fly Neil and me out to Dallas, to be interviewed on one of their shows: 'All expenses paid'. We both thought it was a prank initially, but soon discovered that the man behind the idea was renowned US TV journalist Glenn Beck, who was making a pilot show about inspirational stories. And he wanted us to feature! It seemed surreal. Feeling as though we were pushing the envelope a little, we asked whether we could bring Neil's fiancée, Sarah, as well as two people from Rethink

Mental Illness, Rachel and Natasha. To our surprise, the TV company were so keen to have us that they agreed.

They flew all of us out to Dallas in July, and put us up at the swanky Four Seasons Hotel, where we were waited on hand and foot. All the staff miraculously knew our names, even putting down towels for us as soon as we went downstairs to one of the pools. Getting the full 'celeb' treatment, we had the time of our lives.

The TV show was filmed in front of a live audience, which was extremely nerve-wracking. It soon became clear that the main thrust of our story was very close to Beck's heart, as his own mother had struggled with mental-health issues, and he started to cry during the interview, which in turn set me off. Overall, there was a sense of warmth and support throughout.

A few years earlier, I had started talking online to a guy in North Carolina called Johnny, whose brother, Wesley, had the same diagnosis as me. His family were at a loss as to how to help him, and I think talking to me gave Johnny a better insight into his brother's condition, as well as providing him with some support. As Wesley got better, he too started to talk to me online, and we became friends, of sorts. I had no idea that both he and his brother Johnny were in the audience! During the pre-interview discussions, the researchers had asked me whether I had any connections in the US, and I must have mentioned talking to the brothers, but not for a moment did I expect anything would come from it. When they joined Neil and me on the stage it was a truly moving, special moment. After the show, we hung out together and went out for dinner and drinks, and Neil also became friends with them, an unexpected but lovely added bonus of our trip.

As there were no direct flights from Dallas back to London, we stopped off in New York City and I decided to take a few days off there while the others flew home. A few of my friends from London also happened to be in New York, but our plans never seemed to overlap, which meant that I spent most of my time on my own. Being by myself for long stretches in a different country was a first for me and I didn't handle it well. *At all.* I ended up going from bar to bar, binge-drinking and trying to hook up with people. I felt as though I was starting to crack up again. Back in my hotel room, I scoured dating websites on my mobile in a desperate attempt to find 'someone', oblivious to the enormous roaming charges I was racking up.

By the time I flew back to London, I had to admit to myself that I was very unwell again. My anxiety was getting out of control, and I needed to do something. I decided to see a new psychiatrist, which in retrospect was a wise decision. Despite the fact that I'd spent the past few months working hard to make people aware that they needed to open up about their mental-health issues, I had been too embarrassed and ashamed to let anyone know that I was still struggling myself. I know it sounds ironic, but somehow the #Find-Mike campaign had been such a positive thing; people had seen me in so much better a place than I had been that day on the bridge, that I felt as though I'd be letting them down if I revealed the truth about my current state of mind.

My meeting with my new psychiatrist took place in secret, while my paranoia and intrusive thoughts deepened. Eventually, he put me on Abilify, an antipsychotic drug for which possible side effects include an inability to stay still. Even though not everyone who takes the drug is affected by this, I was. Once the akathisia (constant movement) kicked in, my sleep became badly disturbed and I felt I needed to move my legs constantly. Sitting on a train became virtually impossible.

Once again, I turned to mindfulness, and decided to go on another retreat. This one was in the Cotswolds, which was incredibly quiet and restful in the high summer. Meanwhile, my dad had just been diagnosed with prostate cancer, which meant that while I was coping with mental-health issues, he was struggling with physical ill health. As he started radiotherapy, I felt for him so much, but I was also aware that at least everyone was talking about his condition openly . . . I wondered why we couldn't be just as open about mental health? When my dad first came home after being diagnosed, his oncologist had given him several leaflets explaining what to expect. It really hit home that I'd never been given any information or guidance; there simply seemed to be nothing comparable for mental-health conditions, for the patients or their families. My natural compassion and fear for my dad's health was mixed in with all these other emotions. Fortunately, radiotherapy eventually seemed to prove successful in treating his cancer.

On the retreat, I tried to cultivate my inner resources. On 21 August I wrote:

It's 9.30 p.m. I'm about to go to bed, in a tent, in a field, and it is pissing it down. I couldn't be happier. I feel ten again.

How I wished I could cling on to that happiness! But by the beginning of October, back in London, things were unravelling at an alarming rate. On the Monday before World Mental Health Day, Neil won the Pride of Britain Award for talking me down from the bridge, and the ceremony was televised to millions of people, with comedian and author Russell Brand giving Neil his award. Backstage, realizing how anxious I was, Russell put his hand on my chest and simply said, 'Don't be nervous.' I thought what a lovely gesture it was. When we were finally on stage, I was desperate to hang back behind the others; I was such a mess, the last thing I wanted was to be in the spotlight. But Carol Vorderman, the presenter, gently pushed me forward. People later commented that I looked very fragile, and I certainly felt it. I was so proud of Neil, but I just wanted it to be over. Afterwards, even the backstage banter and jokes from Russell didn't manage to penetrate my mind: my anxiety had trapped me in my own hellish world once again.

I went into the Rethink Mental Illness office the following Thursday and sat down at my desk to read a report my boss had asked me to go through. I tried and tried, but nothing would go in. I went over the first few lines again and again, but my mind had shut down completely. Eventually, I said to my boss, 'I need to talk to you.' He took me into a side room and I became very agitated. I completely broke down, hysterically pacing up and down, bashing my head with my hand. I desperately wanted to self-harm, to hurt myself, albeit not in a dramatic, suicidal way. My boss was fantastic. He called my parents, who were understandably shocked, and put me in a cab home. Even though I insisted nobody travel with me, my colleague Natasha, who has since become a close friend, stayed on the phone to me throughout the entire journey, urging me to tell my parents that I needed to go to hospital.

So that evening I was admitted again, this time voluntarily, and to a different hospital from before.

18

And Down

What the hell am I doing here? How did I end up here?

Diary entry, 10 October 2014

I STAYED IN THAT particular hospital for three weeks. From the beginning, there was a sense of instability about the place: it was so understaffed that at times it felt as though there was no one in charge there at all.

As soon as I was admitted, I was made to tip out the contents of my bag so they could check for anything sharp. I felt no compassion from the male nurse doing this. To make matters worse, I simply didn't gel with the psychiatrist. He kept questioning me about my love life and insisted that if I wanted to get better I needed to find myself a boyfriend and establish a relationship. He also asked me repeatedly about my finances and how much I earned. I still find that shocking to this day.

My entire stay there was a horrible experience. The one saving grace was that we had single rooms. My day consisted of group therapy sessions, as well as various classes, including yoga. A few days after being admitted, while practising yoga, I heard a pleasant Arabic voice in my head telling me to listen to my heart. I was trying, but my head kept overruling me. I found myself longing to be retired somehow, to be old, to be a recluse, but this was impossible, of course. Maybe the pressure was mounting because I knew I would be in the spotlight more than ever when Channel 4 broadcast our documentary, 'The Stranger on the Bridge'. It was still months away, but I couldn't stop thinking about it.

I felt like a shadow of my former self again. Even more so than six years earlier when I had first been admitted to hospital: at least then I had been able to interact with others. Now I was far too anxious to connect. I spent my entire time worrying about what other people thought of me, and this meant that group therapy had become hell. I was convinced that the others didn't trust me, didn't believe me, and thought I was a fake. And yet the psychotherapist, for reasons I still don't understand, suggested that this wasn't a helpful thing to discuss, which heightened my anxiety even further. When everyone got up and left at the end of the session, I felt worse than before: there had been no communication, and the whole experience left me distraught.

Certain memories of the other patients have stayed with me. There was a lady on the ward who suffered from severe anxiety surrounding food. At mealtimes, she would fret, 'Shall I eat fruit now? Should I have a sip of water now?' She would agonize for the entire forty-five minutes that we were allocated for mealtimes. When our designated time was up, we were all simply moved on, which made her terror and anxiety even worse.

On my last night there, we were collecting our 10 p.m. meds as usual when another lady in the queue, clearly distressed, said: 'I'm hearing voices. They're telling me to hurt people.' The nurse who was handing out our medication merely replied, 'I can't do anything about it. Just take your meds and go to bed.' Eventually, the lady became seriously distressed, went into the room next to mine and threw another patient's laptop out of the window.

A diary entry from this time reveals my sad state of mind and that once again I had become increasingly suicidal. On 19 October I wrote:

Today I've thought about dying too many times. If I don't kill myself I'll become agoraphobic. I've thought about that as well today. I've lost the ability to communicate.

Where does this fear of being disliked come from? It's so strong within me, from the clothes I put on in the morning to the way my laces are tied on my shoes. I've come to resent myself deeply.

At the end of three weeks, the psychiatrist told me that if I wanted to be discharged I needed to prove to him that I was well enough to do a whole day's work. So even though I was nowhere near ready, I left the hospital and went to work the following morning. The dread I felt on the train was overwhelming, but I was desperate to leave hospital. Returning that evening, I lied that I had been fine, although going into work had been worse than ever. I was nowhere near better.

After being discharged, I somehow managed to get through three weeks at work, but then, unsurprisingly, I crumbled again. Every day was a battle. I couldn't communicate with people, kept constantly blushing or turning away, wishing the ground would open me up and take me in its arms. It was that beautiful time of the year when autumn arrives and the world is full of shades of reds and browns. Sadly, that also meant that winter was just around the corner and the clocks were about to go forward, signalling shorter days and longer nights. I didn't want to face it. Severely depressed, I was certain that I could no longer go on like this: something had to change. I had no energy, no attention span, and was full of self-loathing. I kept harking back to the past and how I used to be before this paralysing social phobia had developed. I needed to go back to how I had been before.

I'm glad because it's Friday afternoon. I can look forward to two days sleeping and not seeing anyone. It's sad, isn't it? Most twenty-seven-year-olds look forward to the weekends because it means seeing friends or going out and enjoying life. It's so tempting to become a recluse.

. . .

I must overcome instead. If you could see what I see, the setting sun so yellow in my eyes right now. I can conquer this. It restores me. I'm content sitting here staring at the sun.

One day I felt so suicidal that I walked out of work and went straight to the Samaritans. They were wonderful. I had a brilliant interaction with one particular lady there who persuaded me to go back to hospital, even offering to pay for a cab.

What I did next surprises me to this day: I actually called my dad and admitted to him that I was feeling suicidal. He was great, pleading with me: 'Please, please, think about us. Please think about what it would do to us.' So I took a cab home and the following night I wrote:

That was the nail in the coffin, excuse the awful pun. That meant I couldn't go through with my plan. But it's so tempting, it feels so alluring. Death. Peace. Because the day-to-day is so painful. This anxiety never ceases. I keep seeing my funeral. People would get over it. My parents, maybe not. But if only everyone could understand what it's like.

That evening, I was supposed to attend a one-time preview screening of our documentary at PricewaterhouseCoopers, who had permission to show it as a one-off because Neil, who was still working as a personal trainer back then, had a client there. I felt dreadful about cancelling, but PWC were very understanding. After this, I refused to go back to hospital or to work and I didn't even leave the house for a month. I had felt bad before, but not like this for a long time. I was constantly thinking about suicide, and even having the simplest of conversations was impossible. Rethink Mental Illness allowed me to work from home, but in reality I spent most of the time in bed, very depressed and anxious.

I thought about what it would be like if – or rather when – I got my mental health back. One thing was for sure: I would never take it for granted again. Going through old pictures on my phone, I couldn't help but feel that life had been good back then, when I was working in Manchester, surrounded by great friends. I missed that. Right now I felt like a shell, exposed and vulnerable. My total loss of confidence felt irreparable.

I decided to document my relapse journey on YouTube via a series of videos which I called 'Recoverlogs'. However, far from recovering, as time went on I became more and more suicidal, to the point where I was making detailed plans again:

It feels so close. If it wasn't for my parents, I would. I've gone through all the methods. I'm scared of myself.

In December I finally told my parents that I needed to go back to hospital. I had to wait for a bed for a couple of weeks, but eventually I was admitted. This time to a new hospital, a place I'd never been before.

I'm back in hospital again. I could die with dread. I want to die. I should be at the office Christmas party. I should be out, being a normal twenty-seven-year-old, enjoying Christmas revelry, but I'm stuck in here for Christmas and I'm losing myself. I've lost myself already. How do I get it back? What if I can't? I just want out. Out of my head. We can't keep going in and out of hospital. I'm killing Mum and Dad. Oh Jonny, Jonny, what has happened? This time a year ago I was doing ok, and then came #FindMike. I fucking despise myself. How do you recover from that?

Yet from the moment I arrived, this hospital felt strikingly different from the one before: the staff felt far more compassionate, more present, and weren't constantly rushing around or changing their shifts all the time. In addition, I immediately gelled with the psychiatrist (who I am still seeing to this day). She talked in a language that everyone understood, and my parents got on better with her too.

I had been on Lithium, a drug which is usually prescribed for bipolar disorder and, in retrospect, may have caused at least some of my problems. I was now given the antipsychotic Olanzapine again, and this too seemed to help. In fact I settled in quite quickly, even making friends.

The most difficult thing was having to spend the holidays in hospital and having Christmas lunch on my own. The gaudy decorations that festooned the ward only made me feel worse, reminding me that there was a happier place somewhere out there where people were celebrating with their families. However, there was one lovely moment when a male nurse knocked on my door on Christmas morning with a gift – a random act of kindness.

The New Year came and went – 'this has been my *annus horribilis*' – and I was eventually discharged in January. Although not quite out of the woods yet, I felt in a better place. This was not least thanks to the CBT I had started with a new trainee therapist who made a real difference; so much so that I sent a letter to my mental-health trust praising her. Her patience and empathy helped me immeasurably, and I was fortunate enough to receive twelve sessions instead of the six to which I was technically entitled. In addition to the CBT, I was getting back into mindfulness and practising yoga again, and thanks to the combination of this change of lifestyle and the change in meds, things gradually improved. I started to feel less anxious and paranoid and I was finally able to start socializing and reconnecting with friends again.

The following year, 2015, turned out to be a year of recovery. In fact, that Christmas Day I would write this letter to myself:

Jonny, Happy Christmas. I'm so proud of you. This time last year you were sitting in the canteen in hospital eating your Christmas lunch alone. Look how far you've come. You really have.

This time last year you wanted out, never thought you could recover.

And look at you now. Sure, it's a struggle at times, but you've overcome so much. And you will continue to. I want you to feel proud today.

And if you blush around people, you blush. So what.

You're here, and all the family will be together – that is all that matters.

You don't need to perform, just be yourself.

Everyone loves you, unconditionally.

And you must love yourself now, unconditionally, too.

Breathe in, deep, breathe out, long.

There's nothing to fear.

There's only love. Love, love, love. Love everyone, everything and especially yourself today.

I love you so much. And I forgive you. Xxxxxxxxxxxxx

19

Small Pleasures

One of the hardest things about living with my mind is the unpredictability of it. One day I can feel on top of the world, but the next I can barely leave my bed.

Jonny Benjamin, social media message

OVER TIME, LITTLE BY little, I was starting to develop my own coping strategies and even to look after myself a bit more. I had started to treat myself every day by having a hot chocolate with cream and marshmallows in a café while writing. Despite the crippling anxiety I was experiencing, my diary soon became a travelogue of chain coffee shops around London:

> Drinking a soya hot chocolate in the Waterloo Station Starbucks is becoming a pastime. It fills me with relief because the day is so wrought with anxiety. To escape it and be alone feels like bliss almost. I wish it didn't have to be like this, but for now it does. It will change . . .

When you find yourself trapped inside your anxious, depressed mind, even the simplest, most mundane exchange with a stranger becomes fraught with difficulty and a never-quite-defined danger. Going to an anonymous coffee shop, especially one in a train station where the interaction will be limited to ordering a coffee and paying at the counter, feels relatively safe. At this point in my illness, even asking a waiter for the bill would have been an enormous challenge. At the sound of my voice, would strangers raise their head and look at me? What would they think? Just the thought of being conspicuous and exposed to scrutiny scared me.

I have long wondered about how differently people perceive their places in the world. Does the person who man-spreads or who puts their bag on the seat next to them on a busy train or bus feel entitled to that space? Where does that sense of entitlement stem from? Oh, if only I had just an ounce of that confidence. If only I felt safe enough in this world to do something like that. (Well, maybe not exactly like that as it would be inconsiderate and antisocial, but it would be nice to occupy a little more space without fear.)

And I'm not just talking about physical space. The same applies to people who speak loudly on their mobile phones in public, their voice booming as they share personal or trivial information with the same degree of indifference, and without even a hint of self-consciousness. Back then, I couldn't even speak on the phone in an office environment, never mind while surrounded by strangers. What made me so different? The normal things that most people take for granted – like just talking on a phone in public – can be something that people with mental illness find incredibly hard.

And the same goes for eating out. Not long after being discharged from hospital in January 2015, I went to a restaurant with my mum and dad. It was such a mundane thing, something that most people would take for granted, but I remember it because I felt content. I had become so used to feeling anxious and restless that this contentment felt odd. I had an unfamiliar sense that I didn't need anything else; this, just this, was enough – my world felt peaceful for once. I thanked G-d for that moment: if my mind were in balance, my life would be perfect.

Around this time I started working full time for Postcard Productions. Mentally things were still hard. I was back on Tinder, but not sure why: I knew I should be focusing on myself, not a dating app. But I still wanted to find Him. The One. I was still obsessed with the thought that if I could find someone else who loved me, I would finally love myself. Other days I decided I would be just as happy with dogs. Two black Labradors: that was the dream. If I didn't find a man, I would settle down in the country and live out the rest of my years in their company.

In the absence of a man or dogs, I decided to take part in The Alchemy Project, an initiative funded by the Guy's and St Thomas' Charity, Maudsley Charity and Arts Council England. This involved a four-week course, training with a group of young people, most of whom had had psychosis, to dance. This meant going to classes every day in Stockwell, south London. Getting there was tough as I was still very anxious, but everyone was so lovely that I ended up enjoying it. On the last day of the course I wrote:

> I did it. I should be proud of what I've achieved. It's hard to be proud of myself, but I'll try. We did a final performance. It was my first time on stage for seven years. A strange feeling, but I can dance. That's what they told me. I want to do more. I love to dance.

In the weeks leading up to the airing of the documentary, however, I really started to feel the stress. On 11 April I wrote:

> Since we last met I've started Clozapine [one of the strongest anti-psychotics available]. I never imagined I would be on this drug. I'm days away from the premiere of 'The Stranger on the Bridge' at BAFTA [the British Academy of Film and Television

Arts, where Channel 4 showed it several weeks before the actual TV launch] and I'm shitting myself. I'm worried about being incoherent and having some sort of panic attack. My confidence is at the lowest it's ever been, right at the point where I need it the most.

Sitting here in this café, I'm quite content. I could live just like this, but I can't for the moment. I've made a choice and I can't turn back now. I've got dreams. Remember them? The Homeless Dream [I was referring to getting everyone off the streets].

If I give up now how will I ever try and see it through? Do it for Amy.

20

The Screening

ON 4 MAY 2015 our documentary 'The Stranger on the Bridge' went out on Channel 4. We couldn't believe it: our little film, which had been made with virtually no budget, that we had thought was destined for YouTube, was actually on TV. To their credit, Channel 4 were very much behind the project and even gave it a prime slot, at 9 p.m. on a bank-holiday Monday. They were adamant that it was an important subject, and one that wasn't addressed often enough on television. All of us at Postcard, the production company, were immensely excited about this. 'The Stranger on the Bridge' was the company's first ever documentary, and to achieve this level of success so early on was a big deal.

The night of the premiere, the notorious Katie Hopkins tweeted: 'ENOUGH with the ads for #strangeronthebridge. Starting to wish the sympathetic stranger had let him jump.'

Reading that tweet as we were all getting ready to watch the documentary, I felt almost nonchalant; my initial thought was that it simply wasn't worth getting upset about. We all talked about it for a bit, but everyone was too excited about the TV premiere to worry. Nonetheless, there was quite a backlash on Twitter, and Professor Green, whose father had taken his own life, called the tweet 'a new low'. Clearly, feelings were already running high.

Watching 'The Stranger on the Bridge' on TV for the first time was a weird experience. Not only because it told my story, but also because I was one of the producers. We'd had to film new footage for the TV version as it needed to be sixty minutes in length, and it felt as though my professional life and my personal life were colliding. We all watched it quietly, checking our social media throughout and occasionally making comments. The scene which I still find the most difficult to watch is the one where I shuffle through the photos of possible 'Mikes' on the table, my hands trembling, desperately trying to identify the kind stranger. At the time, only a few days earlier I'd sat down with Rethink Mental Illness and said, 'I don't think I can do this any more.' I felt as though I had let people down – the whole search just seemed so futile. And now, looking at those photos, I was forced to relive those scenes on the bridge, my journey there, and everything that followed. Rethink Mental Illness were great, even offering to abandon the search there and then, and this helped me in the end. I felt supported.

There are several scenes which seem to stick in people's minds the most. First of all, the one where I hand out the flyers on Waterloo Bridge, appealing for information about 'Mike'. What is most poignant about the commuters is the way in which they responded; for example, a man who confided in me about his bipolar disorder as we stood there in the cold January sunshine. I couldn't help but be struck by the warmth and openness of their personal reactions – a rarity in London, where people generally tend to be cold and distant.

And finally, of course, there was the reunion with Neil. It was filmed in real time, as it happened, and this is probably why it has such a raw quality, especially the moment on the sofa where everything comes flooding back to me.

The documentary was watched by millions of viewers, and the response was enormous, and mostly positive, especially on social media. My Twitter following jumped up immediately, and we were all inundated with messages: me, Neil, Postcard Productions and

Channel 4. And, just as in the aftermath of the #FindMike campaign, I was once again approached by publishers and literary agents asking for meetings to discuss book deals. But I still didn't feel ready: the time wasn't right.

Meanwhile the feedback went on and on. To our amazement, our documentary was even shown on Gogglebox, and we won various awards, including Best Single Documentary in the Televisual Bulldog Awards, as well as being shortlisted for others, such as the Grierson Trust British Documentary Award. *Radio Times* called 'The Stranger on the Bridge' a 'remarkable, joyous, painful and ultimately life-affirming film', and it was sold internationally. All of this meant an awful lot to everyone involved – my colleagues and friends at Postcard – and to me. It was a big deal for me, and a huge boost.

By the end of May 2015, three weeks after the documentary aired, my mood seemed calm and steady:

No, I'm not sitting in a tea shop for once. I'm actually at home in my favourite place to be right now: in my bed. I've decided to write daily again, in a bid to improve relations with myself. Lord knows it's going to take a lot of work.

I've given up on finding Prince Charming, which is good, as there is no such thing. No, my aim is to love myself, all by myself. And so I start.

All my love

Jonny x

That's not to say that it was plain sailing from here on in. As usual, my moods would suddenly change and I would become overwhelmed by self-doubt and anxiety:

I'm at the mind's mercy. When I became ill at twenty, I still had some respect for myself. I had confidence, self-esteem. These have eroded to nothing. I'm at a loss as to what to do. Those dark moments of depression that used to cloud over me, I used to sit and cry and cry and there was a deep pain, but I would hide it so well. I can't hide this anxiety. Where do I go now? I'm stuck. But I must persevere.

So persevere I did. Only a few days later, on 20 June, I wrote:

Every day has got a bit better since I last wrote. I would even go so far as to say I've had fleeting moments of peace. But there's still a lot of anxiety.

Soon after the premiere of the documentary, I was asked by some mental health-related organizations to give talks about my experience, and that summer I spoke at an NHS conference for the first time. At this point Neil was still working as a personal trainer. After the media storm following the reunion, we saw each other socially a few times, at barbecues or for drinks, but I was still attending the events by myself.

I felt incredibly anxious before the first talk; my heart was racing out of control and it was a thoroughly unpleasant experience. To make matters worse, I was late because of problems with the trains. I ended up running to the venue in east London, and arriving out of breath, feeling like a mess. Yet, despite my extreme internal discomfort, I managed to come across as confident, calm and collected. And the response from the NHS staff was very positive, which made all the difference. To this day, I still get stage fright. I'm very self-critical about public speaking, and hyper-vigilant in terms of people who use their mobile phones or fall asleep during my talks – in fact, a while ago, a psychiatrist was on his phone the entire time, and I became convinced that he was texting derogatory remarks about me, to the point where I started to cry. That got the man's attention! I have also been told that I don't make enough eye contact. These days, thankfully, my nerves generally wear off while I'm talking, and my favourite part is the Q&A section and conversations afterwards, where people approach me and tell me their own stories.

That summer, I was finally starting to feel more like myself. Writing my thoughts down in my diary helped. Yet occasionally I still felt needy and lonely and I still wanted a boyfriend:

> Last night I tried to come on to a chap from the Royal College of Psychiatrists who already had a boyfriend. The night before a stranger took my number. I haven't heard a word. I see people with boyfriends. I want one. No, no, I don't need one. I'm single, free and happy.

I kept vacillating between wanting a boyfriend and trying to be happy on my own, and was constantly questioning both stances. Back and forth, over and over again. Once again, CBT helped, as did a number of personal development courses I undertook during this time, including the Hoffman Process, What If? and the Landmark Forum. Each course was enormously insightful and healing, even though I was still pining for the unattainable, especially during the Landmark Forum:

> I was so good all day, not looking at other men. And then . . . Jack. He's beautiful and sensitive and vulnerable. And an alcoholic, by his own admission. He's been in trouble with the law many times. He also does drugs. I'm not judging. He's got a

good, good heart. And he's a flirt. So when I saw him leave, and I was in the middle of a conversation, I went to follow him.

Follow him I did. I even went for food with him, even though I didn't want it. I want to save him, and help him, and protect him.

What the actual fuck?! You've got to do that to yourself, first, J. Now it's JB's time, not anyone else's.

By September, Jewish New Year, I was looking after myself again:

Shanah Tovah. I'm actually feeling better than I have in over a year. I'm making progress and I'm trying to focus on myself. I've given up searching for a man. The One. A Saviour. All the self-development stuff I've been doing recently has really shown that I need to start being a 'little' (understatement of the year) kinder to myself. I really am trying.

21

Education

I never had any mental-health education at school – I didn't know what it was, or understand the concept of it.

11 January 2016, from an interview with BuzzFeed News

AFTER 'THE STRANGER ON THE BRIDGE' aired in 2015, the guys at Postcard Productions came up with the idea of a legacy project, because the documentary had had such an impact. We all agreed schools would be a good place to start: according to statistics from 2016, 75 per cent of mental-health issues start before the age of 18, and 90 per cent of children experience stigma and discrimination as a result of mental ill health.

This is how Pixel Learning came about, an initiative that runs interactive workshops incorporating film and education, aimed at demystifying mental illness and providing young people with the help and information that they may not be offered elsewhere. This in turn led to the workshop ThinkWell, which was created by Hannah Knight and launched in January 2016 at Dunraven School in south London. Hannah is a friend of Sam Forsdike, one of the founders of Postcard, and had had extensive experience in school workshops. Having visited a few schools to talk about mental health, I had seen first hand that there was a great need for more education on the matter so, unsurprisingly, I was passionate about the project.

On 11 January 2016, the morning of the launch of the project, I woke up to the news that David Bowie had died. I was in shock: another great idol gone. Little did we know at this point that 2016 would see many more celebrity deaths. This one was particularly devastating. All the major media outlets were supposed to cover our launch, but understandably David Bowie's death dominated the news. Only Channel 4 News ran a report. It was a memorable day, but for all the wrong reasons.

Nevertheless, we completed a workshop with a group of fifteen-year-olds at Dunraven. It was fantastic to see them opening up about their mental health rather than shying away from a frank discussion, as I would have done at their age. What we did (and still do) in these workshops is to show the teenagers clips from 'The Stranger on the Bridge', broken up into segments, then engage them in related activities such as drawing, creative writing or role play. These are instructed by Hannah, who has trained up a lot of workshop leaders in the field. The final thing we encourage them to do is write a letter about how they feel, not only about themselves but about others around them, and to send it to their future selves a few months later. We also ask them to put themselves into Neil's and my shoes: what would they have done or felt in our situation? We always take a therapist with us who sits in a separate room (the 'ThinkWell Space') and, although the therapist doesn't listen to what goes on in the workshops, he or she is there for any students who may want to talk to them at any point. A few generally do.

A few incidents from these workshops, as well as from my own talks in schools, have stayed with me. A fifteen-year-old boy once came up to me and confided that he was really struggling, but that there was no way he was going to talk to anyone about it.

'Why not?' I asked.

'If I do I'll never get a job.'

'Where does that come from?'

'My mate told me it goes on your CV if you have mental-health problems.'

When I reassured him that this was untrue, that this would not affect his career prospects, his relief was palpable: 'Oh, but that's why I never told anyone.'

Encounters like these have highlighted for me the need for schools to fight these common misconceptions: the only points of reference many students have (just like me at their age) are films like *One Flew over the Cuckoo's Nest*. These not only give them an unrealistic representation of what it is like to live with a mental illness but they also instil more fear and prejudice.

After another talk, when the Q&A session had finished and most people had left, I noticed a solitary boy of about sixteen standing in a corner of the room. Eventually he plucked up the courage to approach me.

'I've never told anyone this, but I have the same thing you had, when you had to do things in threes, or the devil would punish you. I thought I was the only one. I can't believe it!'

He went on to tell me that his dad had cancer, and that he felt compelled to do things in threes to save him. At the time I reassured him that my own compulsions had more or less stopped: I still hear a voice telling me to do certain things, but I no longer listen to it. I also wrote to him afterwards. It was a complete revelation to the boy that this was a relatively common experience.

Every time I go to a school, I hear similar stories, especially about students being too afraid to talk to anyone, and these stories have made me more impassioned than ever. My ultimate goal is to see mental health embedded in the school curriculum, woven into various subjects. For instance, in history, why not talk about

Winston Churchill's lifelong battle with depression, which he called the 'Black Dog'? We never learned this at school, and neither did we learn about the brain in science. Why can't we incorporate mental health into our study of these subjects, especially as there is so much scope to do so?

I would like to see the Department of Education and Ofsted making this a focus, maybe even teaching all students mindfulness or CBT techniques. On the UK curriculum PE is compulsory, so why not mental health? Once again, there is no parity: mental health appears to be less important than physical health. And because the transition from primary school to higher education can be particularly tough, I believe that mental health should be addressed as early as possible in primary school. While it is nominally part of PSHE (Personal, Social, Health and Economic Education), in my experience students only receive the odd lesson, and these diverse subjects are just lumped together. Sometimes the information is available but doesn't come across effectively. One time, after a talk, several girls told me that they did have a PSHE lesson about mental health, but because they didn't like the teacher they didn't listen. It struck me what a missed opportunity this was.

The week after the launch, Sky News asked me for a live interview. They had seen the press release for the ThinkWell workshops and seemed keen to talk about mental-health education. When I went on, however, all they wanted to talk about was *that* day on the bridge and the #FindMike campaign. Afterwards, frustrated and upset, I went to Hyde Park and burst into tears. How had it all gone so wrong? This wasn't what I had wanted to talk about. Why didn't they understand that it was important for me to highlight the need for better mental-health education and care?

I found that many of the interviews I gave around this time also focused on my suicide attempt and the subsequent search for

'Mike'. It was very difficult to dredge it all up again and again, especially as I'd since had a relapse – something which didn't fit into their neat little narrative of me being 'fine' now. Nobody seemed to understand that things weren't quite so black and white, and that I wanted, *needed* to campaign for a change in the way in which we address mental-health issues, especially in children and young adults, and for better public services in this country. The recurring theme was very much, 'Oh well, you're fine now, so let's talk about that day on the bridge.'

I still shudder when I remember my very first press interview in 2013, after the BBC Three documentary. I spoke to a journalist from a Jewish newspaper while someone from the BBC listened in. To my horror, the story not only made their front page, but I was completely misquoted: 'Jonny wishes that his parents would have done more in his teenage years.'

I phoned my parents from Manchester straight away, and understandably they were very upset. Then I called the person from the BBC who had listened in on the interview, and she in turn phoned the newspaper, only to be told that they could change the online version but that it was too late for the print edition to be altered. To make matters worse, the article also claimed that I was really angry with my old Jewish school and blamed them for what had happened to me, which was simply untrue. Although I have given many interviews since, the experience left me jaded and wary of the media, fearful of being misquoted. I also think some journalists don't really want to delve into mental health in any meaningful way – they only seem interested in either a terrible outcome or a happily-ever-after story.

22

Royal Treatment

In my world, the word inspirational gets bandied around a lot,
but Jonny Benjamin is truly deserving of that adjective.

H.R.H. Prince William, The Duke of Cambridge

IN EARLY 2016, I received a phone call from Kensington Palace.
Being me, I immediately thought I had done something wrong.
Treason, perhaps? I couldn't believe my ears when the lady from
the palace's communications team told me, 'The duke and duchess
would like you and Neil to have a private meeting with them.'

We had quite a long conversation. As it turned out, the young
royals wanted to do some work in mental-health campaigning and
suicide prevention, and after hearing about my story and my work,
they were keen to learn more. The meeting was to take place at
St Thomas' – the very hospital where I had been sectioned almost
exactly eight years earlier. Going back there for a totally different reason felt very strange and, unsurprisingly, I was extremely
nervous when the day came. There were so many cameras from
various news stations in the room, as well as the duke and duchess's team and security. In fact, I was so nervous that I couldn't stop
talking, even while we were still standing, despite the fact that we
were supposed to sit down first. To my surprise, that had been the
extent of the briefing: there seemed to be no rules regarding protocol. On the contrary, when I asked I was just told to 'address them
as you wish.'

Prince William told me that he had watched 'The Stranger on the Bridge' that morning, and Catherine told Neil and me that she thought what we had been doing since was 'really amazing'. Once we finally sat down as planned, William asked Neil how he had begun his conversation with me that day on the bridge, and how he'd known what to say to me.

The first part was for the cameras, then we were left alone to talk, which was even more surreal. There were moments when I had to remind myself that I was talking to the future king and queen of this country! What struck me most was how warm and engaged they both were, and genuinely interested in the subject. Having had personal experience with suicide as part of his work with the Air Ambulance, that was Prince William's main focus, while the duchess was particularly passionate about young people's mental health, and very interested in the school workshops we had started at the time. Both had plenty of questions and ideas on how to improve the situation. They even talked about their own children and how they wanted them to be open about their own mental health. I found it all extremely encouraging.

After the meeting at the hospital, we travelled in convoy to Kensington Palace, in separate Range Rovers with blacked-out windows. Neil and I shared a car with Prince William's private secretary. Everything was timed to the nth degree, each car leaving within forty seconds of the previous one. Travelling through London like this was just as strange and surreal as the meeting itself; it was almost like being in a film.

By now it was afternoon, and we were due at Kensington Palace to meet pupils from Dunraven, the school in south London deliberately chosen by the royals because it was where Pixel Learning and I had launched our workshops. To avoid excessive excitement, the pupils had only been told about their visit that morning. The plan was to screen 'The Stranger on the Bridge', but when we arrived at Kensington Palace, there was a technical hitch and the staff couldn't show it, so Neil and I ended up talking to the pupils instead. There was no longer any press. Halfway through our talk, Prince William and Catherine joined us, and we immediately lost the children's attention: all eyes were on the young royals. Afterwards, as always, I asked whether there were any questions, but by now they were too shy to raise their hands. In the end William stood up and said, 'You should never be embarrassed about your mental health, or to ask for help.' I was very impressed by his impromptu speech, which was clearly heartfelt and genuine.

Leaving the palace and walking through the streets of London, before getting back on the Tube, felt no less surreal than everything else I had experienced during the course of that day. The whole thing felt like a dream.

This was just the first of several meetings I have had with Prince William and Catherine since. The next time I saw them at an event, they made a beeline for Neil and me and asked how we were. I was stunned – I had assumed they wouldn't even remember us. Another time, Neil and I met outside the venue where an event was about to take place, only to discover that we were wearing virtually identical outfits: white shirt, beige chinos, and brown shoes. When Prince William spotted us, he commented, 'You two must be joined at the hip!'

23

Opening Up

It is utterly heartbreaking to see a depressed person who is struggling, only to reply to them: 'Sorry, but the counselling you need is at least a six-week wait'. To this patient, six weeks is 42 days (and nights), 1,008 hours, 60,480 minutes or 3.63 million seconds.

These seconds are not ordinary seconds. Life feels like constantly walking in oversized wellies through knee-high wet mud. It is backbreaking, emotionally draining, gloomy and painful.

J. Ratnarajan, from an article in the *Guardian*, May 2016

ONE THEME THAT COMES up again and again when I talk to groups is how critical that first contact with the GP can be. I was seventeen when I told my GP I was struggling, and straightaway he referred me to a mental-health service. I was lucky – my GP was very good, and took me seriously, but I have heard stories from people who have had vastly different experiences. Sometimes they are simply dismissed: 'It's just a phase, it will pass.'

One woman told me that when she was suffering from depression it had taken her a long time to pluck up the courage to see her GP. When she finally got an appointment, she was thrown by unexpectedly being allocated a different doctor, a locum, instead. Finding it hard to open up to the stranger but afraid she wouldn't get another appointment soon, she told him about her concerns, only to find that he refused eye contact during the entire consultation, staring at his computer screen instead, and rattling off a list of standard questions. She felt just about confident enough to answer the first few truthfully, but when he asked her whether she had a suicide plan, his detached manner made her clam up and answer 'no', even though she had, in fact, already perfected a very detailed suicide plan. The locum sent her away, concluding that she was fine. It was only some months later, when she had to see her regular GP for a general check-up, that the older, more experienced doctor, who had known her for years, picked up on the change in her demeanour. He asked her a few careful questions and then referred her to an NHS counsellor. This lady told me that had her GP not noticed this change in her and acted immediately, her story could have been very different.

It takes a lot of guts to talk about your mental health. It can feel like a massive step and, when you finally take it, it is important to be heard. I still remember the GP at university who told me to change my diet – it felt like a kind of dismissal. To make matters worse, many people still see doctors as authority figures and therefore don't question what they are being told during the ten-minute slot they have been allocated, which is not only inadequate in many cases but also adds to the pressure on both patient and doctor. While GPs are seeing more and more people with mental-health issues, patients are occasionally prescribed antidepressants without being warned about possible side effects, which can sometimes be worse than the original symptoms.

In my experience, most GPs recognize that they need more training in mental health. The training, as it stands, is woefully inadequate. According to the mental-health charity Mind, in 2016 fewer than half of all trainee GPs received a training placement in a mental-health setting, and in 2017 the *British Medical Journal* published an article entitled 'GP Training in Mental Health Needs Urgent Reform', stating:

> We now accept that people's mental and physical health are intertwined, while GPs support more patients to manage complex, comorbid conditions. Consequently, GPs are required to become experts in areas outside healthcare such as housing, relationships, family, and employment, and they must be well supported to take on such roles, including social prescribing.

England, Nash and Hawthorne, BMJ 2017; 356:j1311

Indeed, in 2016 a task force decided that all GPs should have mental-health training. The expectation on GPs to be experts in all sorts of other areas, too, cannot help.

Once diagnosed, a patient may be referred to somebody from the mental-health service, but waiting times are often very long. The lucky ones receive six to twelve sessions on the NHS, but they still end up on a waiting list for more long-term counselling. Many decide to accept group therapy or, if they can afford it, go private. I was talking to a friend recently who has been waiting for a therapy place for eight months. This in itself is bad enough, of course, but when he phones the organization for an update, he feels that over-burdened staff don't have time to explain the situation to him. Even though he tried to take an overdose a few months ago, he still hasn't had any therapy.

Through my work I see these problems again and again. Recently, when I visited a mental-health team in Manchester, they told me how overstretched they were, faced with an increase in both staff cuts and the number of patients on their list. The nurses were literally rushing from house to house to make sure that patients were taking their medication.

According to a task-force report leaked from 2016, the average waiting time for these community mental-health services was thirty weeks. As a result, more and more people are turning up at A&E to seek urgent treatment.[1] Yet when I visited a hospital in Derby in the summer of 2017, several nurses there told me that they had had no mental-health training at all. Furthermore, the environment of an A&E department is hardly suitable for somebody facing a mental-health crisis, as described by a man named James Woods, who wrote about his experience in the *Metro* newspaper on 21 August 2017:

> The wait is often excruciating, and at this hospital, I was sat *[sic]* alone right in the middle of the chaotic A&E ward. This meant I was surrounded by people being rushed in, with beeps and alarms sounding around me.
>
> It's safe to say this wasn't the safest place for me, particularly when I had been brought in by ambulance due to a panic-induced mental health crisis.
>
> But there was no other alternative, and that was the only way I could get the help I needed.
>
> James Woods, *Metro*, 21 August 2017

The harsh reality is that many people who suddenly face a serious mental-health crisis feel that they have nowhere and no one to turn to, and some can even end up in police custody as a result. According to figures from 2015–16, there were 2,100 recorded cases of adults being held in police cells after being sectioned in England and Wales during that period, and although I believe this number has fallen since, the actual overall number of people being sectioned by the police has increased by 50 per cent in the last decade. Under section 136 of the Mental Health Act, the police have powers to remove people from a public space, detain them and take them to a place of 'safety' – which usually means a cell. Unfortunately it seems that police cells are increasingly relied upon as an emergency mental-health service.[2]

And the problems don't always end once patients are released. If there is inadequate aftercare, patients can often end up on the streets: around 80 per cent of homeless people are thought to have a diagnosable mental-health issue. If you think it is hard for ordinary people to get therapy, imagine how much harder it is for homeless people! I do some work with St Mungo's, a homeless charity in London that does outreach work, including checking on people throughout the night. When I turned up there to help one winter evening late in 2016, the volunteers were worried about a young woman they had known for a while who had ended up on the streets after escaping an abusive relationship. She had tried to kill herself the previous evening by taking an overdose, but had been picked up by the police and taken to A&E – from where she had been released back onto the street after a few hours.

I was horrified, but the people at St Mungo's simply said they were used to situations like this. That night, the team and I went to all the places she had been known to go, but we couldn't find her. To this day I don't know what happened to her.

In addition, there appears to be a limited choice of therapy. Although CBT is the most commonly used, it doesn't work for everybody. A one-size-fits-all approach is not effective; in my case, the last time I was ill, several different treatment options were explained to my father, who had a say in the route that was ultimately taken. I now know that this is the exception rather than the rule, however: many people in similar circumstances have no say at all.

I would love the NHS to consider some of the alternatives that I have been fortunate enough to benefit from, such as Compassion-Focused Therapy, which integrates techniques from CBT with concepts from evolutionary and social psychology, as well as developmental and Buddhist psychology and neuroscience. Or Open Dialogue Therapy, which is used more widely in the rest of Europe, including Germany, Italy, Poland and Scandinavia, and in New York. First developed in Finland in the 1980s, at a time when the country was experiencing one of the highest incidences of schizophrenia in Europe, it is particularly effective for people who experience psychosis and/or are suicidal. People are seen within twenty-four hours of becoming ill, and treatment is carried out through meetings involving the patient together with his or her family members and extended social network, usually at home or wherever the patient feels most comfortable.[3]

I have also been working with mental-health trusts on how to increase understanding of the illness within their workforce, to help staff to become more compassionate and empathetic. In the process, I have found that people at a grass-roots level do want to change the status quo and focus more on compassion, despite the lack of funding. In fact, when I give talks, nurses often cry and come up to me afterwards to say, 'Thanks for reminding me why I do what I do.' In my experience, they tend to be very open during our discussions. Some of them complain that they only ever see patients at their worst: 'We never see what happens to them after they leave. It would be important to us to see what difference we made.'

This made me see the need for us to look at the mental health and general wellbeing of mental-health staff, as well as that of their patients: they need to be involved in the bigger picture, rather than just an isolated part of the treatment. On top of that, there is a steady increase in bureaucracy: targets have to be met despite a lack of funding and fewer and fewer beds. During my first mindfulness course in Devon, I discovered that three-quarters of the participants there worked in the NHS, and every single one of them faced burnout. The staff are truly up against it.

On a more positive note, Neil and I have become increasingly involved in events where patients nominate doctors and nurses who have helped them and present them with staff awards. I always find these incredibly moving, not least because the doctors and nurses are so humble. It truly means a lot to them to receive the awards, especially as they tend to be worn down by the fact that the NHS faces so much criticism these days, including in the media, and is woefully under-appreciated.

And it is entirely possible to do things differently. I will never forget the time I visited a psychiatric inpatient unit in Grimsby that was unlike any other psychiatric hospital I'd ever been in. As soon as I walked in, it was clearly an entirely different environment: there was colour on the walls, as well as inspirational, positive quotes and plenty of windows and light. It didn't feel like a hospital. The bedrooms and dining area were homely rather than clinical, in stark contrast to other units, and in addition there was a sense of collaboration between patients and staff – for instance, patients designed the week's menu and cooked it together with the staff. As a result, everyone was more positive and the people working there were very proud of their recovery rates.

The hospital in Grimsby also had a lovely garden, created by patients, and was about to open a garden centre. The public were allowed into the canteen, where patients served them, unlike in other units, which are generally segregated, and there was a real, mutually beneficial integration between community and patients. The hospital even had a 'mental-health bus' to reach people in more rural areas with poor transport links and take them to therapy sessions that they would otherwise have struggled to access. I have served on a number of discussion panels in Parliament, including one with an MP where a member of a farmers' union pointed out the high suicide rates amongst farmers due to a lack of support, probably made worse by their difficulty in accessing services. Yet, as the hospital in Grimsby demonstrates, there are ways of improving the situation. It's not rocket science.

24

In Prison

Our prisons and our jails are now our mental-health institutions.

Hillary Clinton, from a speech at Columbia University, April 2015

AS SOON AS I started to talk publicly about my problems in my YouTube videos, I began to receive messages from people who weren't getting the help they needed. As these messages have increased over the years, so has my awareness of the massive flaws in the current mental-health system. Now, the more public speeches I give as a full-time mental-health campaigner, the more passionate I become about the need for better mental-health services, particularly for young people. This includes trying to get parity between mental and physical health, not only in hospitals and schools, but also in prisons.

Certain cases stick in my mind. After one talk, a mother came up to tell me that her teenage son, who had serious mental-health issues, had been sent more than one hundred miles away for long-term treatment. This meant that she couldn't afford to visit him. She was extremely upset, and who could blame her? It was bad enough that he was ill, but because there were no beds available in her entire county, she couldn't even see him, which in turn made her ill with worry and stress. I've heard this story countless times. Surely if young people are in distress, in most cases it would be in their best interest to be near loved ones? There is an overwhelming sense of helplessness in these families, who feel that the situation is out of their control and that there is nobody to turn to. I can't help but think that if the patient in question had had a physical illness, they probably wouldn't have been sent for treatment miles away from their loved ones. So why is acceptable when somebody has a mental illness?

Other comparisons can be made with waiting times. One teenager told me he'd had to wait for eighteen months for a referral for therapy from CAMHS. Would this have happened if he'd had cancer? Patients and family members aren't the only ones seeking me out to tell me their stories; I also hear from clinicians and nurses from within the NHS, who are frustrated with the lack of resources. To make matters worse, a lot of mental-health services have had to close their books recently, which means that they can no longer take on any new patients.

These days I often speak to staff and managers at NHS Trusts to explore ways of improving the situation for patients. However, the people to whom I really want to talk are those who control the money – such as the Clinical Commissioning Groups. CCGs are generally groups of clinicians within the NHS who decide how the money allocated by the government is spent. Unfortunately, due to a shortfall in funds, mental-health money is regularly 'transferred' to physical health.

As someone who has seen at first hand what lack of funds can mean to vulnerable young people, I have become passionate about doing whatever I can to redress this inequality. I am also fortunate to have had the opportunity to meet some of the people in government, including the Health Minister in 2013, who agreed that the government needed to hold the CCGs to account regarding this allocation of funds. The Health Minister also assured me that there would be 'parity of esteem' from now on, which means that physical and mental health would be treated equally, but again, there feels an awful long way to go until this is fully achieved.

The subject of suicide is the most heartbreaking area of my work, especially when I meet family members or friends of those who have taken their own lives – more often than not because they either didn't get the help they needed, or because they didn't talk about their problems. This is a particularly sad aspect of my campaigning. A lot of charities emphasize the power of talking and it certainly has a place, but what it also needs is to be backed up by adequate services. What is the point of urging people to open up about their struggles when they have nowhere to turn to for help?

In 2016, Prime Minister Theresa May came up with a five-year plan to greatly improve the mental-health system. This is all well and good, but I do worry about those people who are literally dying through lack of help right now. If I could do just one thing in my lifetime for mental-health services, it would be to make sure that money which is allocated to mental health is in fact spent on just that.

As for children's mental health, as recently as October 2017, concerns have been raised about the lack of children's mental-health provision, with stories of desperate attempts, sometimes lasting years, to access support, and even primary-school children raising concerns about anxiety. There are warnings that children's inability to access mental-health support is leading to a range of extra problems, 'from school exclusions to care placements breaking down, to children ending up in the youth justice system.'[4]

Meanwhile, statistics show that 90 per cent of prisoners in the UK have at least one diagnosable mental-health condition. The year 2016 saw the highest suicide rates in prisons on record. The government does not know how many people in prison have a mental illness, how much it is spending on mental-health in prisons or whether it is achieving its objectives. It is therefore hard to see how the government can be achieving value for money in its efforts to improve the mental health and wellbeing of prisoners, according to a report by the National Audit Office.[5] Her Majesty's Prisons and Probation Service (HMPPS), NHS England, and Public Health England have set ambitious objectives for providing mental-health services but do not collect enough or good enough data to understand whether they are meeting them.

Rates of self-inflicted deaths and self-harm in prison have risen significantly in the last five years, suggesting that mental health and wellbeing in prison has declined. Self-harm rose by 73 per cent between 2012 and 2016. In 2016 there were 40,161 incidents of self-harm in prisons, the equivalent of one incident for every two prisoners. In the same year there were 120 self-inflicted deaths in prison, almost twice the number in 2012, and the highest on record.[6]

One story, although just one of many, sticks in my mind. A twenty-year-old man with schizoaffective disorder ran away from home following a prolonged psychotic episode and found himself living on the streets and sleeping next to railway lines. Still in the grip of hallucinations and not aware of his actions, he was arrested and taken to a police cell after breaking into a pub one night and drinking himself unconscious. The following morning, it was determined that he was mentally ill – but he was simply released back onto the streets. He was later arrested again and eventually ended up in prison.

The first time I visited a London jail I was told that an inmate had taken his own life just two hours earlier. I asked the staff how they felt, and their answer was simply, 'We're used to it.' They were sad, not flippant, but this was their reality. I was shocked.

Perhaps surprisingly, some of the best conversations I have had are those held in prisons, mainly because prisoners tend to relish the chance to talk, something which they don't get to do very often. Of course you come across plenty of guys who look incredibly tough, but once I tell them my story they invariably open up. After one talk, a prisoner in his early thirties stayed behind to confide in me. He told me that he'd been in and out of jail for drink-driving and drug offences: 'The thing is that I can't cope with my girlfriend having miscarriages. That's when I start drinking or doing drugs, and then I get arrested.'

Offering him appropriate counselling would not only have been more effective and humane, but vastly cheaper than jailing him again and again, and would break the vicious cycle of him getting arrested, imprisoned and reoffending. Many first offences are committed as a result of substance abuse (which in itself is linked to mental-health issues), as people steal to fund their drink or drug habit. When they are released after three or four years, they are put on an NHS waiting list for support, and it is during this period that they usually go back to self-medicating and reoffend. One of the saddest things I've heard during my visits was prison officers telling me that they remembered some of the inmates as young offenders. Now adults, they still kept coming back, through a 'constantly revolving door'.

As a result of this, prisons are often filled with people who are very unwell, and in many cases getting worse, while incarcerated in these 'concrete jungles', as my taxi driver called one of the jails I visited. Unsurprisingly, they are invariably bleak, surrounded by high walls and barbed wire. During my visits, the strict routine and lack of flexibility always make me feel as if I am back at school, especially the rigid mealtimes (breakfast is at 6.45 a.m.). What is worse, though, is the sense of claustrophobia; the walls seem to be closing in on you while you're in there. Once, when I had finished for the day, I returned to the locker room to retrieve my belongings, and Queen, with perfect timing, came on the radio singing 'I Want to Break Free'.

As mentioned, rates of self-harm and suicide in prisons are high. Officers once told me about a guy who had come in with a plaster cast, claiming he had a broken arm. Soon afterwards he lost a lot of weight after going on hunger strike, and as his arm shrank he was able to retrieve a noose from the cast. Luckily, the cameras picked up on it before he could kill himself. On another visit, the guards told me that one day they had walked into a prisoner's cell to find him holding his own intestines: he had managed to get hold of a piece of plastic and sliced open his abdomen. When Neil asked the officers whether *they* had received support themselves after witnessing something so upsetting, they were surprised: 'No, we're desensitized to it. We just write a report.'

In September 2017 in Wales I spoke to an inmate in his early twenties with schizophrenia who had been hearing voices and going through a particularly bad time. His paranoia had reached a point where he refused to eat the food given to him, convinced that it had been poisoned. Although he had only committed a minor offence, he kept getting into fights with the prison guards. One day the officers decided to let him watch them prepare his food – something as basic as a sandwich – and this simple gesture changed his behaviour dramatically: deciding that they were on his side, he began to trust them, and became less aggressive and far more compliant. What struck me was that something so simple had such an impact; the guy was doing really well now, and I was impressed by the officers' understanding and empathy. The whole episode was incredibly moving as the inmate, who was from a deeply troubled background, told me in great detail what he had been through. The officers were rightly proud of him, but it left me thinking that in some cases prison officers may increasingly, und unfairly, be taking on the role of therapists in the absence of trained mental-health experts.

An officer once told me about an inmate she'd been particularly fond of. He'd committed a fairly minor crime, but two days after being released he took his own life. The officer's words still stick in my mind: 'It's easy to assume that once you leave prison there is freedom, but for some of them going back into the outside world without any support just proves too much and they can't cope. In prison, everything is done for them, their meals are cooked, and they don't have to pay any bills or make any major decisions.'

At the same time, and maybe unsurprisingly, prison riots are becoming more frequent. After the government vowed to come down harder on prisoners following a recent incident, I pointed out in a letter to the Department of Justice that the harder you punish them, the harder prisoners fight back. Unfortunately, one routine form of punishment is isolation, a measurement that affects people with mental-health issues even more than others. Interestingly enough, there is an increased demand from prisons for Neil and me to come back for further talks, but this is always initiated by the prison's management, not the government. Once again, I want to stress that in my experience, the staff in hospitals, prisons and on a community level do the best they can, but it is the system that lets people down.

25

Broken Benefits

THERE ARE ALSO PROBLEMS with the way the benefits system works. The Department for Work and Pensions uses a test called the Work Capability Assessment (WCA) to decide if people can claim benefits such as Employment and Support Allowance (ESA) or Universal Credit (UC). A couple of years ago, a man came to my attention who had taken his own life in 2013, after having been declared fit for work and therefore ineligible for the benefits he had been receiving previously. Originally from Ireland, Michael O'Sullivan had moved to London as a teenager, where he developed mental-health problems including depression, general anxiety disorder, and agoraphobia, and he had tried to take his life before. Although he mentioned all this in his assessment, as well as the fact that he was suicidal again, he was deemed well enough to work. He ended up killing himself hours before starting his new job on a building site.

It was his daughter Anne-Marie, now a campaigner herself, who in 2015 first got in touch with me. His case was unusual because it set a precedent: the coroner, Mary Hassell, ruled that he had taken his own life as a direct result of being found fit to work by the government's disability assessors, and demanded it take action to prevent further deaths.[7]

Anne-Marie told me that her father had been claiming incapacity benefit for a number of years. His combination of mental-health issues all seemed to be triggered after he moved from rural Ireland to London at the age of nineteen. It is a sad fact that immigrants are more likely to suffer from mental-health problems, as a result of alienation and being separated from friends, family and everything familiar to them. Michael O'Sullivan was put through a series of degrading assessments, which he tearfully told his daughter left him feeling 'humiliated, mortified and like a criminal'.[8]

When the Department for Work and Pensions (DWP) refused to offer an apology, Anne-Marie asked me for help with the campaign, and I was very happy to support her. Since then I have looked into more cases of deaths and tried to find out just how many people have died after being declared fit for work. According to figures released by the DWP in 2015, 2,380 people died between December 2011 and February 2014, equalling 90 people a month, but the DWP said no link could be assumed between the deaths and the claimants being deemed fit for work.

Anne-Marie even gave evidence when the UN Committee on the Rights of Disabled Persons launched an investigation. Their findings were damning: according to them, UK welfare reforms had led to 'grave and systematic violations' of disabled people's rights. Findings which the UK government refuses to accept.

This isn't the only controversy surrounding the DWP. Atos and Capita, the private companies they use to carry out assessments for Personal Independence Payments (PIP), which have replaced the Disability Living Allowance (DLA), have also been subjects of much negative attention. With the DWP having paid Atos and Capita an average of £19 million a month over the past two years, the companies are set to be paid in excess of £700 million by the time the contracts hit the five-year mark. At the time of writing, more than 160,000 people initially denied PIP have had this decision overturned since the benefit launched in 2013, according to DWP figures[9], while Atos and Capita have been dogged by accusations of insensitive assessments.[10]

'Insensitive assessments' is putting it mildly, from what I hear. I have listened to too many stories of people with mental-health issues who have been treated appallingly. A friend told me about her boyfriend, who, like me, was diagnosed with schizoaffective disorder at the age of twenty and suffered from severe social anxiety and delusions. He was ordered to attend an assessment in one of the centres in east London, only months after passing a previous interview. Knowing how much anxiety this was causing him – not just the assessment itself, but the journey there and back – his girlfriend offered to accompany him. But she then suffered a panic attack herself caused by stress in the build-up to the day, and missed him at the station. When he arrived for his interview, he was told in no uncertain terms that – as he had managed to travel to east London by himself – he didn't appear to have any mental issues that might preclude him from working. This, despite the fact that he had explained the confusion and was clearly in distress. He ended up having a relapse, but his PIP was still denied.

I have heard this numerous times: if people don't appear for their interview, their payments stop. If they do, they are told that they are obviously well enough to work, and this can have devastating ramifications for their mental health, as reported in the *Independent* on 13 March 2017.[11] Yet the focus tends to be much more centred on 'benefit fraud' and 'scroungers', not helped by television programmes such as *Benefits Street*, or *Benefits Britain: Life on the Dole*, which sensationalize and exploit the poorest in society.

In 2015 I visited the Houses of Parliament for an event with MPs, and I made a point of putting love hearts everywhere I could around the building, especially in the toilets. I Blu-tacked them on walls and statues, asking MPs to 'have a heart' about the WCAs. Then I spotted Iain Duncan Smith, the head of the DWP at the time. He was talking to his aide when I decided to approach him and confront him about the appalling shortcomings of his department. Maybe unsurprisingly, he dismissed everything I said, insisting that Work Capability Assessments were 'working fine'. I was furious. Assuming that I was a journalist, one of his aides escorted me out of Parliament. (I'm surprised I have been asked back since.) Iain Duncan Smith has since resigned from his role, and admitted in 2017 that WCAs given to sick people are 'too harsh and offer a cliff-edge choice between work and no work.'

Too late for some, including Michael O'Sullivan. It just feels as though there is no justice, especially as the situation is ongoing, not only for people with mental-health issues but also for those with physical disabilities. In 2016 a blind man had his benefits axed because he couldn't read the letter the DWP sent him, meaning he missed his assessment. His brother appealed on his behalf, but he was still deemed fit for work. It's not just the lack of compassion, it's the lack of common sense which infuriates me, particularly given that a study carried out by the National Audit Office found that the assessments were likely to cost more than they saved, as reported in the *Independent* on 8 January 2016.[12]

26

Isolation

Nobody Knows You When You're Down and Out

Song by Jimmy Cox, 1923

THE STORIES I HEAR about loved ones shutting themselves off from the world are, after stories of suicide, the most heartbreaking. Wherever I go, people come up to tell me that they feel they have 'lost' their partner, parent, sibling, child or friend because they either don't want to talk about their problems or are simply too unwell to do so. As a result, their loved ones feel terrible too. This, of course, is what happened to me.

One young woman told me that she had no option but to become a carer to her brother after he became so paranoid that he decided to live in the shed at the back of their home. She did his washing, brought him food and generally looked after all his needs. She couldn't get any mental-health professionals to visit him: the decision to get help would have had to come from him, but he refused to leave his shed. It was devastating to see how helpless she felt, trapped in this hellish cycle, with no end in sight and nobody to support her.

Another story, which was featured on Radio 1's *Newsbeat* in November 2016, really struck a chord with me. It was about a woman whose twenty-eight-year-old brother, an aspiring musician with schizophrenia and bipolar disorder, had been sleeping rough, and she found herself unable to get help for him. By all accounts, he was talented and, like me, had had a book of poetry published, but he had started to self-medicate with drink and drugs following psychotic episodes and suicide attempts. Sometimes his sister didn't see him for weeks, not knowing whether or not he was still alive. One quote from her was particularly upsetting: 'Last time I saw him he had a big red mark on his forehead; he said people had been kicking him in the head. He had blisters all over his hands. Someone had set fire to his mattress and he'd burnt his hands.'

She strongly believed that sectioning him was the only way to get him the help he so clearly needed. Every time she contacted social services, the police or charities, she hit a brick wall. According to Dr Philip Timms, a former NHS psychiatrist who was also featured in the programme, there is a 'scandalous reluctance to use this power [to section somebody] in the homeless community'. He also pointed out that in 'most cases arranging to have a homeless person sectioned will involve coordinating the police, social services and medical staff so they are all in the same place at the same time. And if there are no hospital beds available, the whole process will be for nothing.' The sad reality is, as Dr Timms went on to say, 'You have a person with a severe mental-health problem living on the street and they will die on the street unless something is done about it. That is a form of medical emergency. It's scandalous that we leave very vulnerable people on the streets for months, years and sometimes decades.'

So what are the family and friends of a homeless person with a severe and potentially life-threatening condition to do? And how must it affect them, knowing that their loved one is out there – ill, exposed to the rain, cold and, even worse, abuse? The effect of a mental illness on a family member or partner is not widely recognized, and as a result there are few resources available to them. If somebody has cancer or another potentially terminal condition, their loved ones are involved at every stage of the process, and given advice and support from organizations such as Macmillan Cancer Support. Who do you phone in the middle of the night when, as one woman told me, your partner is in the grip of a psychotic episode and punching holes in the walls, threatening to kill himself if you have him sectioned? Who do you turn to? This woman told me that on many occasions she frantically googled 'support services for partners of schizophrenics UK' and repeatedly came up with a blank, as the only support groups she found tended to be based in the US.

Similarly, my parents didn't know what to do when I was first diagnosed. I had been very good at hiding my illness from them until that December in 2007 just before I was sectioned. On my arrival at the private hospital (the one from which I would later escape), my parents were coolly asked whether they had insurance – 'If not, we take credit cards' – before being forced to witness me having all my belongings taken from me so that I couldn't kill myself. As the doctors didn't share any information with them, they were still in the dark about my diagnosis, and found it difficult to explain to people why I was in hospital. What do you say? If I had been admitted with a broken leg it would have been so much easier.

That January, when my dad got a phone call informing him that I had run away wearing just a T-shirt and jeans, confusion and helplessness turned into shock.

Eventually he asked me, 'What happened on that bridge?' and I tried to explain about the stranger. In the absence of any supervision at this hospital, my mum was thinking how easily I could run away again.

Over the following weeks, while I was sectioned, I didn't really want to engage with my parents about my mental-health problems.

Being in group therapy was hard enough, and when they came to see me I wanted to hear about the outside world. For the first few years after my diagnosis, as a family we didn't know how to talk about it. Now I know that my mum felt a strong sense of guilt about my diagnosis – as far as she was concerned, and from what she had gleaned from the media, people with mental-health problems came from broken homes. When I experienced my first hallucinations after watching *The Big Friendly Giant*, my parents understandably assumed these were nightmares, and being so young myself, I didn't have the understanding or vocabulary to explain what was happening to me. Later, at school, teachers would tell my parents in my school meetings how well I was doing. There never seemed to be a problem – the teachers liked me and I had a lot of friends. Although inside I did feel very alone.

Like many of us who struggle with mental-health problems, for a long time I was able to hide that part of my life. My parents didn't even know that I was writing poetry until I read out one of my poems at my maternal grandmother's funeral. Neither did they know about the YouTube videos I had started making in 2010, under an alias. It was only when a family friend stumbled across one of them and told my parents that they became aware of them. They watched them before telling me, and at first I was shocked – I'd thought this was something I could keep secret from family and friends. (None of my friends knew about that day on the bridge before the #FindMike campaign. I told them just before it was launched, and only because I had to.) What must my parents think of me? Wracked with anxiety, I wondered whether I should stop, but then I decided that it was a good thing they'd seen them: surely they'd understand me a little better now? As it turned out, what they found most shocking was the fact that I'd kept all these things a secret.

The whole YouTube revelation kick-started a shift in my relationship with my parents. As I'd never been able to sit down with them and talk face to face, this was the first time they'd heard my story properly, in all its raw glory, and now the channels of communication were finally open. This doesn't mean that any of this has been easy – my mum still occasionally struggles with guilt, and I only found out later how hard my diagnosis was for even my brother and my sister-in-law – but at least now we can talk about it.

My parents had to find out for themselves, the hard way, how to deal with my mental-health issues. Like many carers, they were unsure how to access help and support, partly because there are so few resources out there, and partly because of a common misconception that the term 'carer' only applies to those who look after us in an official capacity. These days, armed with much more information, they are incredibly supportive and often come along to events. My dad even gives talks on the subject (and his experiences with me) and has appeared on a BBC feature with me about fathers and sons. In addition, both he and my mum cut out articles about mental health and always tell me about relevant TV programmes or news stories. Just recently my dad told me that during a routine visit to his GP, the doctor had confided in him about her own son's struggles with anxiety and my dad ended up giving her advice on how to get help! Since my dad's appearance on *BBC Breakfast*, friends and colleagues of his have approached him and opened up about their own children's or other relatives' mental health, and he always gives them advice.

One thing we talked about on *BBC Breakfast* was how men, in particular, find it difficult to talk about their emotions, and how doing something different, like talking in the car, can help. You don't always have to talk face to face; that can feel inhibiting. When asked by people how best to broach emotional or mental-health issues with loved ones, I recommend writing letters. Not only does it give you time to choose your words carefully, but you can do it in your own time, in a safe space, whilst giving the other person time to digest the information before they react.

All this feels very different from the confusion and ambiguity that used to surround my illness. I feel very lucky to have had a lot of support from family and friends, something that became particularly obvious during my last relapse in February 2017. This time I was able to be much more open with them about what was going on and, in turn, it was easier for them to deal with everything.

Yet even with all the information in the world, being close to somebody with a mental illness can be challenging. According to an article in the *British Journal of Medical Practitioners* from 2010, research into the impact of care-giving showed that 'one third to one half of carers suffer significant psychological distress and experience higher rates of mental ill-health than the general population. Being a carer can raise difficult personal issues about duty, responsibility, adequacy and guilt.[5] Other reports indicate that depressive symptoms are twice as common among care-givers as in non-care-givers.

Another issue that needs to be addressed is the lack of support for those who have been bereaved by suicide. After a talk I gave recently, a woman in her twenties came up to me and burst into tears. I discovered her husband had taken his own life and she had been waiting for therapy for a whole year. I was shocked, but unfortunately not entirely surprised. I hear this far too often from people who have been left with no information or support after a loved one's suicide, despite themselves being at a much higher risk of depression or suicide, as they struggle to come to terms with what has happened. Once again, it is left to third-sector organizations to do all the work, usually charities such as Survivors of Bereavement by Suicide (SOBS), who run support groups all over the country. And then there are some smaller ones like Durham-based If U Care Share, set up by a woman called Shirley Smith who lost her own son to suicide. This seems to happen quite often: people who have been affected by the death of a loved one set up charities to help others in similar situations.

Partly due to social problems, which often go hand in hand with mental-health conditions, it can be hard to maintain friendships when you are unwell. In many cases stays in psychiatric hospitals are considerably longer than for physical conditions, and this is when you really need people around you. Sadly, this is also when friends tend to fall by the wayside. In my case, I was lucky that many stayed, but every time I felt that people had disappeared from my life, especially during the period when I couldn't come out much due to either anxiety or IBD, it hurt. Then I'd listen to Nina Simone singing 'Nobody Knows You When You're Down and Out'.

It was partly the anger in the lyrics that resonated with me then, as it does to this day – not just because of my own story, but because of those I have heard about since. Despite the fact that these stories often make me angry, I really enjoy meeting other people with mental-health issues. I always feel an affinity with them, a real connection.

I got a chance to do this when my friend, the campaigner and author Bryony Gordon, set up 'Mental Health Mates'. This is a regular meet-up for people who are finding life difficult, where they can walk together and talk without fear of being judged or stigmatized. I joined them on a walk on Clapham Common in south London and was struck by how amazing it was to have these open and honest conversations with others, safe in the knowledge that nobody would think any less of us. There was a lovely lady who told me that she hadn't been out of her house for ages: 'This is my first time for several weeks.' I felt a huge amount of empathy and admiration for her. There are a lot of amazing people out there, people like Bryony, who set up these extraordinary initiatives with no public funding. And that is another issue; the fact that in the current political climate, they are forced to do so by themselves.

I am also really proud of the work I have done with JAMI (the Jewish Association of Mental Illness), and especially the work they've done in combating the stigma around mental health within our Jewish culture. From creating a mental-health-themed Shabbat/ Sabbath, in which many synagogues now take part, to opening up a mental-health café called Head Room, in Golders Green at the heart of London's Jewish community, they have made huge strides in the last few years. I've been to many Jewish schools and synagogues with them to talk openly about my own mental health. Recently I did some work with the orthodox Jewish community, which is something I never imagined possible! And in 2016 I won the Topland Award for all this work, a prestigious award that has been given to the likes of Sir Nicholas Winton in the past. I often get asked about combating stigma in other communities, such as the Black and Asian ones. I always say it is possible. I've seen it happen within the Jewish community; it can happen anywhere else, too.

Although there is always more work to be done, campaigning can be very effective, even at grass-roots level. Early in 2016 I was shocked to hear that The Bridge, my own local mental-health centre in Harrow, was going to be closed down because the council could no longer afford to keep it open. I was horrified: the centre, which Neil and I had visited together for a talk, was supporting hundreds of local people in the area, including families and carers. I had also attended some of the groups there, including one which focused specifically on paranoia, and found that they were doing excellent work. They also ran a variety of activities such as creative writing and art classes.

What the council hadn't counted on was the opposition they would have to face once we started our campaign to save The Bridge from closure. People who relied on the centre's services worked night and day, writing letters, collecting signatures, standing outside shops on freezing-cold winter days. With 1,775 signatures under our belt, we marched to Harrow Civic Centre where the council are based, singing 'Save the Bridge', a song that one of the members, David Phelops, had written.

The reaction we received from the council was not the one I expected. As we were standing there outside the building, several councillors emerged from the building saying, 'We want to join you!' before taking song sheets and singing along with us. Afterwards, they invited us inside and listened to everyone's views. Maybe for the first time they could hear personally and in detail about how the closure of The Bridge would affect people's lives, and how much they would suffer as a result. Many of the service users would be forced to travel for miles, often under extremely challenging circumstances, to access help and support. Life would become very difficult, not just for those with mental-health problems but for their loved ones and carers too.

To my amazement, the councillors listened and took everyone's input on board and, as a result, The Bridge was saved in April 2016. As the then council leader, David Perry, commented in the press at the time: 'I have personally visited The Bridge and come to understand this is a lifeline to many and that service users rely on the activities there to improve their quality of life. With mental-health facilities closing across the country due to devastating government cuts to councils, I am immensely proud that we have found a long-term and sustainable future for The Bridge, after tireless work by campaigners and council staff.'

I was surprised and stunned by their decision, especially after seeing so many other places being closed around the UK. The mere threat of losing the centre had already started to affect the mental health of people who relied on it, so the news that it would stay open came as an immense relief.

27

India

Compassion is the radicalism of our time.

Dalai Lama

AFTER BECOMING SO FAMILIAR with the UK healthcare system, it came as a great surprise when I had a chance to see at first hand some approaches to mental health in other cultures and countries.

At one of my talks I met a woman named Miranda. 'You may be interested in some of the work I do in India,' she said. She went on to explain that she ran the UK branch of a charity called Snehalaya, meaning 'home of love'. It had helped a lot of vulnerable and disadvantaged people, especially women and children in India. At the time we met, they were running a huge campaign called 'Her Voice', with the aim of empowering women in India who had been the victims of abuses such as rape and forced marriage. Their headquarters are in Ahmednagar in the state of Maharashtra, 120 km northeast of Pune, where they have a huge facility that houses hundreds of children, most of whom have either been orphaned or abandoned.

'It would be great if you could visit the place and meet the children,' Miranda suggested. 'Their physical conditions are being treated, but not their mental-health ones.' Of course I jumped at the opportunity – Snehalaya's work sounded extremely impressive, and I was keen to see for myself.

I arrived in Mumbai with Miranda and a few volunteers from the NGO. Everyone had warned me that India would be a culture shock, but I wasn't prepared for the overwhelming intensity that hit me as soon as we left the airport; all these different smells, sounds and sights. It was the busiest place I'd ever seen: there were the constant sounds of car horns as every driver seemed to make up his own rules while avoiding the many cows wandering in the middle of the road; the motorbikes, seemingly the most popular form of transport here, whizzing past at great speed; the sound of market traders calling out; the intense smell of spices in the searingly hot and humid climate. The level of poverty also became quickly visible; there were beggars everywhere, including young children who clearly lived rough and were wearing hardly any clothes.

Exhausted from the flight, we still had a six-hour drive to Ahmednagar ahead of us. The scenery was mostly barren and dry countryside and mountains, the bumpy roads very different from the ones we are used to in the UK. We overtook countless buses crammed with people. Everything, including the vehicles, seemed somehow much older than at home, and I didn't see a single woman driver – they all appeared to be travelling on the back of motorbikes or in tuk-tuks. I would later find out that very few women drive in India.

When we finally arrived at the facility, our car swung into a massive courtyard and we were greeted by a large crowd of smiling children running up to us. They were so excited to see a Westerner that they hugged me straight away and held onto me for ages, asking, 'What is your name? Where are you from?' It was touching to see how friendly and warm they all were. I found out later that there were a large number of people living on site who looked after the children, both girls and boys, from babies through to teenagers. Eventually we were shown to our dormitories which, although somewhat spartan, were perfectly comfortable: there was a bed, table, bathroom, and small kitchen area, all in a separate building. Built from scratch by the charity, Snehalaya, and situated on the outskirts of the city, the facility also housed a large school and a healthcare unit for those who were seriously unwell.

Exhausted after the long journey with its myriad of new impressions, I wanted to go straight to sleep, but our wonderful, welcoming hosts insisted on taking us to a local restaurant. There we were treated like royalty, and this really set the tone for the rest of the trip, as people loved to take care of us. Everyone was asking me a lot of questions, calling me 'John Brother', keen to learn more about mental health, and I was struck by how positive they all were. I found out that the volunteers were all from a variety of backgrounds, while the people who set up the charity were mostly philanthropic businessmen who remained involved and caring. Despite my overwhelming fatigue, I couldn't help being in awe of the whole enterprise.

The people from Snehalaya had organized a packed schedule for us, mostly focused on mental health and involving various facilities and projects that they were running, looking after the most vulnerable members of society. They were also the first to admit that mental health was not something they had focused on so far. I was shocked to learn that India has one of the highest teenage-suicide rates in the world, with more females than males taking their own lives, in contrast to what happens in the rest of the world. While I was there, a young girl was brought in with 70 per cent burns to her body after trying to kill herself. As Snehalaya didn't have the appropriate facilities to treat her, she was transferred to a hospital. Tragically, she died five days later.

Despite all this, there was a lot of fun and laughter at the facility. One of the great joys of my stay there was watching the children dance. I also witnessed some great work being done throughout India and met incredibly inspirational people, including at another facility run by Snehalaya called Anamprem, where deaf and blind students were given a chance to study. Their motto was 'Disability is not Inability'. How true this is!

Unfortunately, I also saw things that really troubled me, including a mental hospital with long-term residents. On the main ward, I saw bed after bed filled with women dressed in red robes, their heads shaven. The director, who it transpired was a physicist with no background in mental health, explained to me that once his patients were admitted they would stay there for life, never to be let out or discharged. Shocked by what I was hearing and seeing, I decided to secretly film my visit. One of my encounters was with a young woman of about nineteen, who seemed entirely *compos mentis*.

'How long has she been here?' I asked the director.

'About eight months.'

He went on to explain that, like me, she had been diagnosed with schizoaffective disorder and sectioned following a psychotic episode, her first. It struck me that she didn't belong there. She was completely lucid, and yet she had been sentenced to a life in a mental hospital, with no hope for release. It was heartbreaking.

When I pressed the director further, he explained that his patients were merely medicated twice a day, but received no talking therapy and were never allowed to go outside. During the day, they were simply left to their own devices with nothing to do, no education or activities. I spent some time talking to the women, and watched them doing henna tattoos on each other's arms – one of the few activities they were allowed to engage in to fill the emptiness of their days. Some were clearly heavily drugged, but others were entirely rational. The director proudly showed me the new extension they were building, thanks to a 'generous' donation of one million dollars from the Rotary Club, in order to accommodate the ever-growing number of patients. Of course the numbers were growing because nobody was ever discharged. This troubled me greatly. Surely there had to be a better solution than this?

He told me about another patient, Lolita, who had escaped through a ventilation shaft twice and, as he was happy to relate, had been caught twice. He was laughing as he told me the story. As taken aback as I was at the time, I'm sure he wasn't a bad person – he simply didn't know any better. He was genuinely proud of his hospital and believed that he was saving these poor women from a worse fate, pointing out that many of them had been raped and would end up on the streets if discharged. When I told him my own story, he was incredulous. He refused to believe that it was possible to recover from psychosis, despite the evidence to the contrary, and the fact that I was sitting there right in front of him. When I asked the director why there only appeared to be women in his hospital, he replied, 'If a man becomes mentally ill it's more acceptable. However, if a woman does, her role in society – as a wife and mother – goes out of the window.' In short, she lost her value.

If I had thought the main ward I had visited upstairs was as bad as it could get, I was sadly mistaken. On some level I must have suspected that worse was to come because I had the presence of mind to pretend I had a call coming in so I could continue recording in the additional ward which was downstairs. This was where patients were held when they were admitted and needed to be assessed. And when I say 'held', I mean in cages. Drugged up to the eyeballs, including women with children. It didn't seem humane. Once again, surely there had to be another way? Yet every time I tried to challenge the director about the recovery aspect, he became very defensive and insisted that no such thing was possible. The sight of children running around the hospital was particularly sad.

This was the only life they knew, behind bars, through no fault of their own, or any fault of their mothers. In fact, many of them had been born there, and even called the director 'father'.

In the end, just like in the rest of the world, good mental health-care boils down to affordability. I also visited some great private hospitals in India where patients were receiving excellent care in their own private rooms; it was the most vulnerable and poorest people of society who ended up in the state- or charity-run facilities with no hope for a better life.

From the hospital, we went straight to a temple where people 'dropped off' family members who were mentally unwell. To my horror, I discovered a man chained up in full view of visitors. When I asked why, I was simply told, 'He's crazy.' As it turned out, he and others in his dismal situation had been left there in the hope that faith healers would exorcize their 'demons'. The almost medieval image of this poor man in chains, exposed to the stares of random visitors, haunted me for a long time.

However, some of the other places I saw during my trip were filled with joy and hope. I spent a day in Pune visiting the Schizo-phrenia Awareness Association, set up by a father whose daughter had schizophrenia and who was determined to allow other children with the condition a chance to take part in therapeutic activities such as creative dance, yoga, art and meditation. This centre was doing such amazing work that it was hard to believe it was only a few miles away from the temple where people were kept in chains. In stark contrast, this place was so light, airy and friendly, and it was wonderful to see the people there express their experiences with mental illness through creative dance.

I really want to go back to India and do more work there to raise awareness of mental health, help improve treatment and reduce suicide rates. As it stands, suicide takes 700 lives in India every single day. Even in a country with as large a population as India, those figures are staggering. There is so much we can do to change this, but we can only do it by working together.

In a country where homosexuality is still illegal and gay men are called 'MSM' (men that have sex with men), Snehalaya also do a lot of work with the LGBT community. They took me to meet a secret gay men's group on the very same day that people in London were celebrating Gay Pride, and there I was, sitting in a darkened room with a group of men, many of them married, who were forced to hide their sexuality as though it were a dirty secret. It felt very strange indeed.

After talking to the group, we went to a local bus station. I was told that this was where 'MSM' came for sex. Desperate for a wee, I went to the urinal, only to discover a man waiting there. Let's just say I hurried up with my wee. The whole situation was extremely awkward. Around the back of the station, outside the toilet, the ground was a sea of condoms. I thought at least it was good they were using them. My guides told me it was an open secret that this was where 'everyone' came to have sex.

After that somewhat uncomfortable experience, we went to meet a group of transgender women living in a secret flat. Keen for a little levity, I was delighted to discover that they were hilarious. One of them took a real shine to me and insisted she was coming home to the UK with me as my bride. They were all very chatty and funny, but the dark reality behind all this frivolity was that they'd all had to run away from their families. There were about fourteen of them living in a fairly small room, but what shocked me most was the revelation that every single one of them had self-mutilated: when they lifted up their saris, I saw that they had cut off their penises. Needless to say, any 'follow-up treatment' they'd had was a backstreet affair, as were their boob jobs. When I asked how they made a living, I was told via my interpreter that it was mostly through prostitution. Despite the language barrier they were all very interested in what I was doing, and we had some great conversations.

The one I took to most was the youngest. Only fifteen, she was covered head to toe in burns: I found out that she had tried to kill herself. When she talked about her experiences, I was touched to see how supportive everyone in the group was towards her: it was clear that they were all looking out for each other, and Snehalaya was trying to keep them as safe as possible.

We also visited the slums, which horrified me just as much as the hospital and the temple. Row upon row of makeshift tents, with piles of human and animal faeces at each end. Pigs running around, people living in their own waste; the occupants seemed to be mostly women and children. I had a chance to play with some of the kids, and discovered that they had no chance of education. The tents, which 'housed' about six people on average and mostly consisted of rags, were packed together so tightly that the sense of claustrophobia was overwhelming, as was the pervasive stench of human waste. There was no way of escaping it, it was everywhere, and I realized that no matter how much people had told me about this, and how much I'd seen in documentaries, the reality was so much more shocking than I could ever have imagined.

There was one moment in India that has stayed with me ever since. One night in the children's home in Ahmednagar, I was sitting outside the main building with a boy of about eight or nine when he turned to me and said, 'I'm really, really cold.'

'Why don't you get a jumper?' I suggested.

'There aren't any left,' he replied.

I couldn't help thinking that when I got cold as a child I would simply ask my parents for a jumper or a jacket without giving it a second thought. How much we take for granted. One thing is for sure: I will never forget my time in India. I will never forget all the incredible people I met, particularly the young people whose courage and determination inspired me.

When I returned from India, I reflected a lot on how much I have, not just in terms of material possessions but in terms of family, friends, and even simple things like being able to have a shower whenever we want to. And although our mental-health system needs an urgent overhaul, it is still far better than in many other places.

28

Mates

Jonny: It's really special; it's unlike any other friendship.
Neil: It's a proper bromance.

AFTER BEING REUNITED FOLLOWING the #FindMike campaign, Neil and I only saw each other sporadically at first – usually when we were being interviewed or featured in the media. That changed when we went to Texas to appear on American TV: now, for the first time, we were actually spending time together and, as we began to talk about personal matters, I felt like I was really getting to know Neil.

When we returned to the UK, we fell back into our old habits, just meeting up occasionally, usually to get drunk together. The fact that I was once again going through a difficult period and heading for a relapse didn't help. I didn't really want to meet anyone during that time, but then people started asking us to give talks together.

Our first joint talk was in Grimsby, for the NHS, and it couldn't have gone any better. We even received a standing ovation. I realized that we were working well together: the talk had flowed naturally, and we bounced off each other on stage. This was a real high for us both.

Afterwards we celebrated with fish and chips on the seafront and ended up getting drunk in a karaoke bar, downing 'fish bowls' – huge glasses filled with various liquids and spirits (G-d knows what, but one thing is for sure: they were cheap and contained rather a lot of artificial colours). Neil was keen to do karaoke, so I signed him up to sing, but they wouldn't let him as only locals were allowed. At the time it was funny, because we were so pissed.

Despite these shenanigans, we took our talks, which started to happen every few months, very seriously. Then, at the end of December 2016, Neil told me that he wasn't happy in what he was doing for work and needed to change career. He was thinking about becoming an estate agent. By now, people were commenting that there was a lot of banter between us. So, after thinking it over I replied, 'We have something quite unique here in terms of our story and our talks, and we always get incredibly positive feedback. We've been to companies like Goldman Sachs, HSBC and others, and it's always been a success. Maybe it would make sense to turn this into a full-time job for both of us?'

We embarked on our new joint venture in January 2017. Around the same time we became creative directors for AWARE in Hackney, north London, a space that mental-health organizations and charities could use for free. We both loved the concept, especially at a time when so many charities were losing affordable spaces. In addition, we were busy raising funds for the London Marathon, which we had decided to run in aid of Heads Together, the young royals' mental-health charity, with a target of £100,000. We were also booking regular talks.

We started out managing everything ourselves – we didn't have a PA at the time, and soon the work seemed endless. Our friendship was put under quite a bit of strain, not helped by my relapse a month or two into working together. Soon after my recovery, the pressure to meet our marathon fundraising target mounted. Even though we were pushing ourselves harder and harder, we weren't doing terribly well. At the same time, ever more people and organizations were asking us to give talks, to support them or become involved in their projects. We simply didn't have the resources to do it all.

Because we were running the marathon together, there was renewed media frenzy about our friendship. LADbible, a social media and entertainment company, made a video about us that got millions of views, and suddenly there was a media response from around the world, including the *Washington Post* and a running magazine in Canada.

Around this time, we were scheduled to give a live interview to a radio station in Chicago. Talking about the day on the bridge, Neil said, to my horror, 'It was really cold, but obviously not as cold as where you guys are in Canada.' I elbowed him, and there was a deathly silence at the other end; just the sound of tumbleweed blowing. If this had happened to me, I would have wanted the ground to open up, but Neil was utterly unfazed. His self-assurance, and the way in which he perceives his place in the world, is something I aspire to: he is unfailing in his confidence and lack of embarrassment. I believe that this lack of self-consciousness is the reason why he came up to me on the bridge in the first place.

After the media frenzy following the marathon died down, it was back to reality. We were inundated with more requests than ever, and having to deal with everything ourselves, on top of doing a lot of travelling, was exhausting. Not to mention the talks themselves, which force me to relive everything and can be very draining, to the point where I sometimes say to Neil, 'I can't face going through all this again.' Then, after the talks, people often come up to me to talk for up to an hour. Many of their stories are so harrowing that they stay with me for a long time afterwards, but despite all this I do find it incredibly rewarding.

Adding to the pressure is the fact that people often comment how great it must be that we have become friends. Some even assume that we must have 'such a wonderful life together'. The reality is that – as with all relationships – things aren't always so easy or black and white in real life. At times working together so closely is a struggle, and leads to conflict – of which there was certainly some in 2017.

One thing I've noticed recently is the very rare talent Neil has for making someone feel heard and understood. Particularly young people. When we visited the Welsh prison together, I wasn't surprised at how great he was at talking to the prisoner with schizophrenia: he is so personable and empathetic that people warm to him instantly. I often feel moved when he talks to youngsters who are struggling with their mental health, and he tells them that they are inspirations for speaking out and getting help. I don't think he realizes the difference a few kind words can make to people. I can see in their faces what it means to them when he speaks to them so positively and encouragingly. I suppose that's the way he was with me on the bridge.

Neil's self-assurance is a gift. He passes it on to other people when they doubt themselves. Not only does he have a very patient and empathetic way of listening, but he also has a way of speaking that can really lift someone up. We joke and banter and he calls himself 'one of the lads', but in reality he's actually very – dare I say? – spiritual. I believe that, at least. Maybe a better term is wise. He certainly comes out with powerful words of wisdom in our Q&As. People in the audience occasionally come up and tell him he is my guardian angel. Neil always says I inspire people, but I think he inspires people just as much by what he did that day. It took more conviction and courage than I believe he perceives. He calls it just being human. But in this world we live in, it is kind of superhuman to do what he did.

I also admire how he has embraced his new role. After we were reunited, he could have walked away. He could have said, 'I've done my bit,' and that would have been the end of it, but he embarked on this journey with me. A journey which, despite the often saddening stories we hear, and the hard work that is still ahead in our quest to improve mental health, not just in this country but globally, is also filled with laughter.

No matter what conflicts we have – and let's face it, whenever people are thrown into close proximity together, they are bound to get on each other's nerves at times – I will always remember one thing. Neil, out of all those other people on the bridge, stopped to help me that day. And what he has been doing since then has been very bold and brave and extraordinary. Sometimes I forget and then I remind myself.

I will be forever grateful.

29

Triggers

I think I'm beginning to like myself.

Diary entry, 3 November 2017

JANUARY 2017 WAS A significant month for me: both my parents had just celebrated milestone birthdays, I had been awarded an MBE, and my thirtieth birthday fell on the 31st. Arguably even more momentous was the fact that it marked nine years since the time I had tried to take my own life and Neil had saved me.

However, during the weeks leading up to my thirtieth I started to struggle again. Insomnia reared its ugly head but, despite my exhaustion, I found it impossible to turn down engagements. Neil and I were incredibly busy travelling around the country, giving speeches and raising money for the London Marathon. My sleep patterns became increasingly erratic and I found myself lying awake night after night, compulsively checking my social media. Most of the comments on YouTube and Twitter have been supportive – many of my followers have either experienced mental-health problems themselves or are close to somebody who has – but of course you always get the odd troll. And now, after having been awarded the MBE, they became even more vocal. The taunts ran the gamut from, 'You've sold out. You shouldn't have accepted it,' to, 'Jump off the bridge already, wimp'; these lone voices sounded so much louder than the ones from my far more numerous supporters. Against my better judgement, I continued to engage with these people, refreshing my browser again and again, only to be tormented by more taunts and insults.

By the time my thirtieth came around, I was exhausted and manic. I had arranged a night of celebrations in Shoreditch for a group of friends, including a cocktail-making class in a private members' club, and karaoke, but as the night progressed and the drinks flowed, I realized that I had vastly overstretched myself, both physically and financially. And of course I had the hangover from hell the following morning. I was clearly not looking after myself.

On Valentine's Day the following month, Neil and I flew to St Andrews in Scotland to give a talk at the university. Although we'd expected hundreds of students, only about five turned up. Nevertheless, it still went fine. Afterwards we stayed up late drinking far too much, and encountering drunk groups of students in various states of undress roaming the streets. So this was what they'd been doing while we were giving our talk! These students from one of the country's elite universities, from which none other than our future king and his wife graduated! Luckily, Neil and I saw the funny side.

Unsurprisingly, I felt rather fragile when we arrived back in London the following day but, true to form, I had booked a full day of meetings. We were already running late by the time we landed, and on the train from the airport to central London I became increasingly paranoid and self-conscious, convinced that everybody was watching me. I even started to suspect Neil and asked him to put away his phone, worried that he was texting my parents that I wasn't well. During the weeks leading up to this, Neil had expressed concerns about my mental health, but I had made him promise me not to tell anyone. Now he was begging me to cancel our meetings, but I was having none of it. It was a classic case of me trying to do too much and my mental health suffering as a result.

When we arrived at Victoria station, I checked my phone and found yet more tweets attacking me over the MBE, and questioning why I had chosen to go to Waterloo Bridge during rush hour, suggesting I was an attention-seeker. One particular nasty tweet pushed me over the edge, and I snapped.

Over and over, I asked Neil, 'Why do people hate me? Why do they hate me?'

Neil tried to calm me down, once more suggesting we cancel our upcoming meeting in Covent Garden, but I was so manic that I refused, despite the fact that it was becoming increasingly obvious that I had crammed too many appointments into our already tight schedule.

When we finally arrived, the receptionist mentioned that we were running late. Now, timekeeping has never been my strong point, and her casual remark, on top of everything else, was the final straw. Before I knew it, I was on the floor, screaming. No words, just screams. I don't know for how long this went on, but I remember running out into the street at some point, embarrassed at what had just happened, leaving Neil inside the building with our suitcases. I was still in hysterics when he caught up with me. By now I was right back at square one, with the whole cycle starting up all over again. I became convinced that I was the star of my very own *Truman Show*, and I screamed at Neil that he was just an actor, that it was all false.

As I became more and more caught up in my psychosis, laughing one minute and the next begging him to get me out of this, I was aware of people watching us, with one guy in particular staring and laughing. 'I need to call your dad,' Neil insisted, but I stuck my fingers in my ears and kept repeating, 'I'm a good person, though.' I paced back and forth on a street somewhere in Covent Garden, speaking those words like an unstoppable mantra, while Neil was on the phone to my dad, who told him that he needed to take me to hospital. By now I wanted to go back to Waterloo Bridge, just a short walk south through Covent Garden, and throw myself off. My psychosis was taking me down the same old rabbit holes as before. Neil tried to flag down a cab and bundle me inside, but I threw myself on the ground again, still hysterical, refusing to go to hospital.

That first day on the bridge, my depression had been stronger than my psychosis, but now it was the delusion that had me firmly in its grip. Nothing Neil said could get through to me – until he hit on a new idea: 'Let's go to this restaurant I know.' Unwittingly, he was echoing his suggestion of years ago that we should grab a coffee together. Deep down, I knew that this was a ruse, but when Neil flagged down another cab, I agreed. I was beginning to understand that I needed to be somewhere safe. Ironically, noticing my erratic behaviour, the cabbie was reluctant to take me, muttering something like, 'Oh, if he does anything funny . . . ' but this only made me determined to prove him wrong, and I began to calm down. I guess you could say he had used reverse psychology, albeit not intentionally.

So Neil took me to a hospital nearby. My dad had phoned ahead, and they had a bed ready for me, which was lucky. As we got there, I still insisted that I was fine, that I didn't need to be there, but I did feel calmer once I got to my room. When I was eventually able to take stock, I realized that on top of using social media obsessively, I hadn't always taken my medication at the right time and had skipped meals as well as my mindfulness exercises. They gave me a lot of sleeping pills and I finally caught up on much-needed rest. And my psychiatrist banned me from social media. But, as I reminded her, my MBE ceremony was coming up, and I needed to be out for that.

Since that latest relapse, I have made a conscious decision to focus more on self-care. As I become more aware of how I can stay healthy, I have identified three triggers that can contribute to a relapse. The primary one is not getting enough sleep. I tend to have a lot of nightmares, or extremely vivid and disturbing dreams, often about going back into psychosis. Sometimes my thoughts race before I go to sleep and when I wake up in the middle of the night they are still racing. When I finally wake up properly in the morning, I feel as though I've had no sleep at all. Making sure I get a good night's sleep is vital.

Another trigger I need to try and avoid is stress. To a certain degree, it is unavoidable, of course, but I have a tendency to pile work on myself and worry about things incessantly. I'm finally beginning to accept that I can't manage a heavy workload, and I try to be OK with that.

Finally, alcohol. We all know that it is a depressant, but it also affects your sleep, which means that it is the last thing I need. I'm getting so much better at managing that. It can seem as if a drink is a great way to unwind, but I realize that for me it is likely to pile on more stress and complication. Identifying these triggers and managing them as effectively as possible is vital for me to maintain good mental health.

That doesn't mean I don't still occasionally push myself too hard. Recently, Neil and I had travelled to New York to talk to companies there and meet charities. I became concerned because the suicide rate is now at its highest in thirty years in the USA. Each year, more than 44,000 people take their own lives there. I also learned that they are in the midst of an addiction crisis, particularly among young people. One thing that everyone we spoke with seemed to agree on was the importance of early intervention, and prevention through mental-health education. They were excited to learn of our mental-health workshops in UK schools and urged us to bring them across the pond.

Personally I found our speaking engagements in New York challenging. It was my busiest month ever, coming on top of a trip to Northern Ireland and Canada. I was already exhausted by the time we arrived in the Big Apple. During one corporate talk my brain seemed to completely shut down. It was almost as if the cogs of my mind stopped turning. I had given this talk hundreds of times and knew it inside out, and yet here I was speechless in front of this audience. I was mortified. Thankfully, Neil did a brilliant job of rescuing the talk and explaining to staff that this was exactly the reason we all needed to take care of our own and each other's mental health. I was fearful this could happen again in our next and final talk in New York, but it turned out to be a great success. Many members of the audience shared that they had never heard anyone talk so candidly and openly about mental health, and it appeared to really affect them. I realize even more how lucky we are in the UK to have wonderful organizations such as Time to Change, who have been groundbreaking in reducing stigma thanks to their incredible 'Champions' – individuals from all walks of life who have shared their own battles with their mental health.

I have also been helped by the Compassion-Focused Therapy (CFT) I've been having. A while ago, somebody recommended I should look at the work of Kristin Neff, a leading self-compassion researcher and associate professor at the University of Texas, Austin. It struck a chord: previous therapists and psychiatrists have always picked up on how self-critical I am – the idea of self-compassion has been alien to me for as long as I can remember.

I am often asked for advice on the best forms of treatment for conditions like mine, and one thing I can say is that it's good to keep an open mind and try all different kinds of therapy. In 2016, I attended a CFT workshop presented by Charlie Heriot-Maitland and Eleanor Longden, which was specifically aimed at people with psychosis. I was interested after watching Eleanor's incredibly well-received TED talk 'The Voices in My Head', which told the powerful story of her own diagnosis with schizophrenia. It has now been viewed over 4 million times on YouTube. At the height of her own illness, in a desperate attempt to get rid of the voices she was hearing, she came very close to drilling a hole into her own head. Thankfully, she went on to make an amazing recovery. I found her truly inspiring, and the two-day workshop she put on with Charlie at King's College, London, with about thirty participants, was utterly fascinating. Afterwards, I spoke to Charlie, and subsequently saw him for one-to-one therapy. For the first time, I found a therapist to whom I can say absolutely anything without feeling as though I am being judged, safe in the knowledge that I am heard, listened to, and understood. Another thing I like about CFT is that it is not purely focused on the self, but on compassion for others as well. The whole experience has been a huge milestone for me.

One method that Charlie uses involves placing different chairs in the room. Then, when a difficult situation from your past comes up, he first makes you sit in the chair of the self-critic before moving on to another chair where you speak from a place of self-compassion. It may not work for everybody, but for someone like me with a background in drama and acting, playing different roles feels very comfortable. I find it immensely useful. This therapy is certainly very different from others I have had in the past, many of which felt very clinical and made me feel awkward. Unlike 'normal' social interaction, the conversation tends to be rather one-sided (the patient talks while the therapist listens, throwing in the odd remark or question), and I used to want to ask my therapist how *their* week had been, or just engage in small talk. It's very different with Charlie: I have no hesitation in asking him questions or chatting, and he is absolutely fine with it.

He also reminds me that it's not my fault my brain is working in a certain way – it's just how it has developed. It helps me separate myself from my mind, and this too has proved incredibly helpful.

As a result of the CFT, now when I meditate I do so with a much greater degree of self-compassion. Every time I get anxious or distressed, I try to use a method called 'soothing touch', which involves giving yourself compassion by stroking a part of your body. Or I practise 'positive self-talk' while looking into a mirror – significantly different from the past, when I would concentrate on every single thing I thought was wrong with me. These days I also keep a 'self-compassion log', where every night I list positive things I have done during the day, often just little things that have pleased me or made me proud. I have come to realize that all this needs to be a constant practice: when I keep up my meditation, self-gratitude, and writing in my diary, I feel much more at ease with both myself and other people. When I neglect these routines, my mental health deteriorates.

In a similar vein, the psychiatrist I see these days works in a welcoming, friendly environment – again in contrast to others who have treated me in the past. There is always at least one vase with bright flowers in her room, and her desk is a huge sea of thank-you cards. She also wears a lot of sweet-smelling perfume that pervades the room, and again, this makes me feel comfortable.

When I had the relapse in 2017, the first thing she said was, 'Look, it's not your fault,' and, 'you're going to get better.' The relationship I have developed with her means that I can rely on her.

And I am getting better, despite the odd bump in the road.

30

Vulnerability

ONE ASPECT OF MENTAL illness that I find very troubling is just how vulnerable it can make people. For instance, recently I have been troubled by certain memories from my twenties. They involve meetings with older men that were disturbing, and have left me wondering whether they've had an impact on my relationships. These range from a very traumatizing event when I went on holiday with a big group of friends and someone forced me to be sexual with him, to some exploitative experiences I had when I was in my early twenties and in the grip of a delusion that I could make it as a model. I wasn't working properly or earning decent money, so when people suggested I try modelling I decided to give it a go.

I found two different photographers who had advertised for models for their portfolios. They each arranged private sessions to take pictures of me. Striking the usual poses first then saying, 'You look great, but if you're serious about this you need to take your top off. Modelling agencies want to see your whole body.' I was flattered: they were so encouraging. Then they asked me to take my jeans off, and then: 'I really want to take a shot of you with your pants off.' I felt I couldn't say no: portfolios were expensive and they were taking these pictures for free. In my mind, they were doing me a favour, really, so surely I should return it? In hindsight, it seems shocking how easy it is to get drawn into this kind of exploitation, but my lifelong difficulty in standing my ground certainly didn't help matters.

Both experiences were jarring to say the least, but it was the second photographer who still bothers me the most. I travelled halfway across the country to meet him, in a cottage in the middle of nowhere. I realize it seems naive in hindsight, but I often wondered whether all this was engineered – he must have known that I was a fish out of water, miles away from home, with no way of even getting out of there without transport. Before I knew it, his boyfriend had walked in on the shoot, and they coerced me into being sexual with both of them. I was truly scared: they were both a decade or two older than me and physically very strong. There was no way I could have fought them off. It was a frightening experience, and I was grateful I didn't end up getting raped.

It's been on my mind ever since that both these photographers must have taken lots of pictures of young men – boys, really. How many of them went through what I did? The thought troubles me. The recent allegations about people in the public eye show that it is important to make sure men know they can't do these things to women or to men. How many more stories are we about to hear about men abusing their power? Just recently, I surprised my parents by joining them on a trip to Israel. One day I went to the Dead Sea when a much older guy came on to me in one of the pools. We'd just been chatting when he began to slide one hand up my leg and said, 'Let's go to the showers.' Shocked and flustered, I told him I had to meet my parents. I'm still exploring with my therapist how much of an impact these experiences have had on my mental state, but I strongly suspect they have contributed to the fact that I often struggle with being touched.

There are other aspects of my illness that also make me more vulnerable, such as when things don't happen as I expect them to: I always imagine worst-case scenarios. I think people are dead if they show up late or don't communicate with me for a while.

I know it's irrational, but it's my go-to thought. I also convince myself every illness I get is going to cause my death. A few years ago, after being exposed to really loud music when I worked as a photographer's assistant in my mid-twenties, I developed tinnitus. I convinced myself it was a brain tumour, and even managed to persuade a specialist to give me a brain scan. When the scan didn't show up with anything, I told myself that my results had got mixed up with someone else's. It seems funny looking back on it now, but at that time it just felt so plausible!

Ever since I was young I've felt that I have an almost sixth sense of when people are looking at me. I get this sense, particularly on the Underground, that someone is staring at me. And when I look in their direction I find that they are. Maybe I'm being over-sensitive, but it jars with me. Strangers looking at me can deeply unsettle me. I always imagine that they are judging me negatively.

I also feel guilty all the time. I used to reply to every single comment on my YouTube videos and every private message. But now I can't. I just don't seem to have the time, especially as I have become so busy with my awareness work. The guilt about not replying haunts me sometimes, and it's difficult to tune out.

Social media is another minefield – or maybe a better analogy is that it's a double-edged sword. Although it's a fantastic tool, it can cause us a great deal of anxiety. I worry once I've posted something. Is it going to offend someone? What will people think? But then I worry when I don't post anything for a while. Will people think I've stopped caring? It's a vicious circle.

Just recently I've been getting pangs of anxiety when I open Instagram and look through people's photos. There was one someone posted of me recently at a mental-health event which got very few likes compared with other pictures from this event. Getting trapped in my own hamster wheel of obsessive thoughts, I couldn't help but feel insecure. Full of self-doubt. And at times I wonder whether I expose too much, share too much, especially on YouTube. I can't bear to watch my videos back. The more I become trapped in this obsessive train of thoughts, the more I worry that people think I'm selfish and self-obsessed. I don't think I'm selfish, but I do think I can be self-obsessed. The deeper I dwell on these dilemmas, the harder I find it to come up with answers.

I know that I am extremely sensitive, which means I can fly into a blind rage in a matter of seconds. But it annoys me when people use the term 'snowflake' to describe sensitive types in order to shame them. When did being sensitive (and compassionate) become a bad thing? I also often think that I'm a difficult person. I set my expectations of others and myself so high that I become frustrated if people don't think or act in the way I expect. At the same time, I've been told that I'm rubbish at accepting compliments or praise. I think it's because I'm afraid that my reply will come out as fake or insincere. So I often don't tell people the nice things I really want to say to them.

My thoughts run like this incessantly. And sometimes it bothers me, but then I remind myself of the psychiatrist R. D. Laing's assertion that insanity is a perfectly rational adjustment to an insane world.

We grow up believing in a Disney-like universe where everything has a happy ending, only to discover that the real world is not a fairy tale. Nobody has prepared us. I don't think that it's a coincidence that my first delusions occurred around a great loss (the death of my grandmother) and then going to a bewilderingly large secondary school. I can't help suspecting that hearing the voice of an 'angel', or believing I was starring in *The Truman Show* was a refusal to accept the harsh reality of the world around me.

What really makes me sad, now, is how long I believed I was hopelessly crazy and insane and that somehow I had to find out the truth about my illness all by myself. I wish every single person struggling with their mental health had the same chances I've had, to peel back the layers of their diagnosed mental illness and discover what experiences in their past could have led to their emotional state today.

I wasted so much time in my early twenties lamenting my sorry state and wishing I could return to the person I was pre-diagnosis, but in recent years I've realized that a return is simply not possible. Letting go of that dream and accepting where I am and who I am now has provided a huge relief.

31

Achievement

This is an evolution neither of us saw coming.

Neil Laybourn

I RECEIVED MY MBE on 28 February 2017. After having been discharged from the psychiatric hospital only a few days previously, it felt totally surreal to suddenly be at Buckingham Palace. The whole experience seemed almost dream-like: the splendour of the palace, the pomp, the ceremony, and then the actual moment I received the medal from Prince William. I was incredibly nervous. There was a protocol to follow, and I was sure I would get it wrong. But during the ceremony Prince William gave me a broad, warm smile as I walked up to receive my medal and put me at ease immediately. He asked where Neil was, and I pointed to him in the crowd, at which point Prince William waved to Neil and to my family who were sitting with him. The whole room turned around to face Neil and my family, which was rather amusing.

As always, Prince William was incredibly kind about my work and very sincere in congratulating me. I felt uneasy receiving the medal. Before the actual ceremony I'd met with other medal recipients and some of them had done thirty, forty, fifty or more years of service in their specific fields. I felt embarrassed to say I had only been working within mental health for a few years. But when I walked away from Prince William, medal in hand, I felt a rare sense of pride and had to stop myself bursting into tears. It was all rather emotional.

When we finally left the palace, it felt like stepping out of another world. It reminded me of my previous visit with Neil. What made me happiest on this occasion was having my mum, dad, brother, sister-in-law, and Neil, all there to witness the event and be a part of it. It simply wouldn't have been the same without each of them there.

Almost exactly two months after receiving the honour, Neil and I were due to run the London Marathon. The night before I slept fitfully, tossing and turning, constantly checking the time. At 5.30 a.m., deciding there was no longer any point in trying to sleep, I got up. I was supposed to have a suitable breakfast ahead of the run, but I was so nervous I couldn't eat.

The past couple of months had been difficult to say the least: my uncle had passed away, followed by my paternal grandmother just a few days before the marathon. At that point I didn't even think I would be able to run; I hadn't had any opportunity to train and, worse still, my grandmother's funeral was set for the day of the marathon, although in the event it was moved to the Thursday before. That Friday was my mum's birthday, and the Saturday was my twin cousins' Bar and Bat Mitzvah. It's fair to say the run-up (excuse the pun) to the marathon had been an emotional one, and the media interest added to both the excitement and my nervousness. My highlight was a tweet from J. K. Rowling, who commented on a piece in the *Telegraph* about Neil and me running the marathon: 'This is a beautiful and extraordinary thing.'

The morning started off terribly grey, but brightened up on the journey there. I was still nervous, but the other runners on the train helped. When we arrived at the starting point, it was already crowded with people and I started to get quite excited. As we were running for Heads Together, Neil and I had been invited to a special reception in a tent ahead of the actual marathon. Prince William and Catherine were there, and talk quickly turned to how fantastic it was that people had finally started to open up about mental health. The first thing Prince William said to me was, 'Jonny, I'm so sorry to hear about your granny.'

I was touched that he knew my grandmother had just passed away, but also pointed out that he, Catherine and Prince Harry had done a lot of work over the previous few weeks. Prince William dismissed this, rather humbly I thought, and replied, 'No, it's you guys who've done all the hard work.' Both he and Catherine were really lovely and encouraging.

Very soon afterwards, we had to go to the start line, and off we went.

The original idea was for Neil to run ahead – after all, he used to be a personal trainer, whereas I had done next to no preparation. As advised, I'd had a big bowl of pasta followed by a bath the night before, but that was the extent of it really. We'd also both made the mistake of googling stats on the internet and discovered that unless you finished in eight hours or less, you had no chance of getting a medal. Still, there we were, and I was determined to keep up with Neil and complete the run at a good pace, no matter what.

We completed three miles, then five, and I was still keeping up. After the ten-mile mark, we looked at each other and said, 'Well, we've made it through about a third, so maybe we can finish together.' As we were running through south London towards the centre of the city, the crowds were getting bigger and bigger, and the noise was growing: everyone was cheering on the runners. The atmosphere was electric – people from all ages and backgrounds were supporting us, encouraging us to keep on going. Some of the children in the crowd were really young: I remember a boy of about four chanting my name (they were displayed on our shirts), and I thought, 'Why can't we do this all the time; why can't we always support each other in this way?' There were all these strangers lining the streets of London, handing out sweets and oranges to us. Towards the finishing line, there was even wine and beer, really the last thing we needed at this point, but it was a sweet gesture. There were also people from many other different mental-health charities, including Rethink Mental Illness, cheering us on.

After about seventeen miles, Neil started getting cramps in his legs. 'I need to slow down and stop and stretch,' he said. 'You run on.' But I insisted we stay together. There was still a long way ahead, and Neil could no longer run properly; in fact, he was reduced to jogging at this point, at times even walking. Ironically, although I hadn't trained, I was still going strong; it was almost as though my legs weren't my own. I had to keep on moving.

At two points on our route, Neil and I spotted our families: Neil saw his wife Sarah and her mum, and I noticed my parents, brother and sister-in-law. Seeing them spurred us on. Eventually we ran across Tower Bridge and from there westwards along Victoria Embankment. Suddenly Waterloo Bridge came into view, and there was a sense of wonderment. This moment was by far the most poignant one, and so overwhelming that we both remarked on it. 'Nine years ago we stood on it under very different circumstances, and now we're running under it!'

Then we ran past the Houses of Parliament towards the finishing line, which is just beyond Buckingham Palace. This was the hardest stretch: I was unbelievably exhausted, but determined to stay under the 5 hour 30 minutes mark that was getting closer with each step. And we did it! The sense of elation and relief as we crossed the finishing line, hand in hand, was incredible.

After we received our medals, we went to a post-marathon reception hosted by Heads Together. For the next few days, my legs were crushingly sore, and I was covered in blisters, but I felt such a sense of achievement, heightened by the surprising – and unexpected – media coverage afterwards. I received calls from all around the world, including Australia, Canada and the US. I had done it!

The only question now is, 'What can I do next?'

32

Neil's Story

It was emotional. In truth, it could have been anyone who stopped that day. It could have been the person behind me, but this time it was me.

AS I CROSSED WATERLOO Bridge on my way to work that cold January morning and I spotted a young man sitting on the railings, dressed in just jeans and a T-shirt, looking towards Big Ben, I had no idea that what was about to happen would eventually change my life.

Originally from Watford, I had moved to London only a couple of months earlier. Life was good: I was dating Sarah (now my wife), and had just started a new job as a fitness trainer in the West End. I was working long hours trying to build up a client base, and my commute from Teddington was not an easy one, but there was so much to look forward to. The future looked good.

As I walked towards the young guy on the bridge, I started to realize that this was far from good. I looked around to see whether he was with anybody, but he seemed to be alone. People walking past him stared at him, but nobody stopped. I knew instinctively that I had to do something, so I approached him carefully.

'Hi mate, are you all right? Why are you sitting on the side of the bridge?'

'Can you go away, please? Leave me alone!'

'No, I want to know why you're on the bridge.'

'I'm going to kill myself.'

'Can I ask why? Why do you want to kill yourself?'

'I can't live any more. I can't be here any more, it's too painful. I can't deal with life any more.'

'Can you tell me what's going on?'

'I'm not well.'

The next thing I remember from the conversation was me trying to find out more about his illness. I needed to engage him, but he was having none of it.

'Can you please just let me do this? Don't try to stop me.'

I thought, 'OK, let's try to find out a bit more,' so I asked him where he came from.

'I ran away from hospital.'

'Which hospital?'

He told me it was in Stanmore or Harrow – I don't remember which.

'Really? Where exactly? I grew up near there.' I told him I was from Watford.

This was the moment when something tipped. I'd been chipping away, and now, suddenly, it was as if a switch had been thrown. He looked at me for the first time and engaged.

'Really, did you?'

Now, we finally started having a conversation. I was debating whether I should grab him, but decided that should be the last resort. Instead, I stayed calm and reassuring, thinking, 'I'll deal with the shit storm afterwards, let's just deal with this right now.'

Still, nobody else had stopped, except for this one guy who looked back at me and raised an eyebrow, as if acknowledging the situation. I've often wondered whether he was the one who called the police. In the meantime, I asked the man on the edge of the bridge about his family, and he said that nobody knew he was there. I decided just to let him talk, which he now did. Eventually I suggested we have a coffee.

'There's a Caffè Nero at the end of the bridge, let's go and talk some more. It's freezing, mate.'

The guy turned, his hands still clutching the railing. Finally he started to climb over the side of the bridge. For a while he just stood there on the pavement, looking dazed, but we both knew we were going to have that coffee. Just then, out of nowhere, a police car came screeching up. No sirens. The young guy immediately panicked and tried to jump back on the edge of the bridge, but I grabbed him with both arms and held him back.

After they handcuffed him, his head down in the car, the police officers took my statement. They were terribly matter-of-fact, completely unemotional, as though they couldn't care less about what the guy had just been through. I asked them where they were taking him, and they just told me, 'To hospital.'

From there I went straight into work mode and into a training session. I didn't explain why I was late; in fact I didn't tell anybody about the incident for quite a while, except for Sarah. In hindsight, that was the worst thing I could have done. But I thought the police were dealing with it, the guy had his family – how would I have been able to help in any way? I tend to think deeply about things, and I internalize them, which means questioning them, doubting them, comes naturally to me. How did my actions that day affect him? By thinking about it deeply, I felt as though I was owning it consciously, and I didn't want to talk about it until I had processed it. In addition, as I hadn't been in my new job for long, I didn't know people there well enough to mention it. I did, however, talk to Sarah in more detail a little later.

I never tried to find Jonny, but for years afterwards I felt guilt. It was a philosophical question: did I change the man's destiny by doing what I did? He told me how unbearable his pain was, and that he needed it to stop – did he now have to live with it still? In some respects, even though he didn't jump, the whole episode hadn't ended terribly well: the guy was hysterical, crying in the back of the police car. I hoped he would find peace. It was me who stopped his journey that day, so I hoped he would be OK.

Some of this only really came to the fore after meeting Jonny again. Before, my only frame of reference was that one conversation on the bridge, but since our reunion my perspective has changed. At the time, talking wasn't a concept open to me – which is ironic considering the work Jonny and I now do, including with the police, who understand that they have training issues and need to handle these situations more sensitively.

I don't know how, but the whole #FindMike campaign completely passed me by. It was Sarah who happened to see a Facebook post on the train home from work. By now we were engaged and living in Surbiton. It was around 10 p.m., and I was about to go to bed when she phoned me. I was shocked: it was the last thing I ever expected. After Sarah got home, we clicked on the link in the post and I was immediately transported back to that day: I recognized Jonny immediately from the photo in the piece. When I read all the media coverage and comments on social media, I was shocked to see how many people claimed to be me! Which meant that now I had to send a convincing email – after all these false leads they were bound to scrutinize every single word. But I had to do it that night; I couldn't have slept a wink otherwise, there was such a sense of excitement.

Rethink Mental Illness got back to me very quickly; in fact they either called or emailed the following morning, I can't remember which. I was struck by how enthusiastic they were; they wanted to meet up as soon as possible. Rather poignantly, the first meeting, with Natasha and a colleague, took place in the very café where I'd suggested Jonny and I should go that day, at the end of Waterloo Bridge. The second time we got together, this time in Covent Garden, they told me that they were convinced I was genuine, and that they were filming a documentary. 'Now we can draw this to a conclusion,' they said. They were both very emotional.

I've often been asked whether I was nervous about being filmed, but I was confident, thinking, 'What you put out into the universe, you get back.' And I had a lot going on at that time: work was busy (I was self-employed), and I was organizing boot camps with several employees as well as sorting out my wedding. Above all, I was excited to meet Jonny: I wanted to show him what a positive guy I was. I was willing it to be a positive interaction, and I really wanted to meet Jonny's expectations.

On the day of the reunion, having been told how nervous Jonny was, I decided to be the opposite: Mr Cool. What I remember most is having flashbacks to the day on the bridge as Jonny talked. I was in listening mode. The connection between us was back, and when we hugged, I was sure that we would be friends. Everyone there was very emotional.

Since then, our friendship has evolved. In fact, as I mentioned on a recent trip to Belfast where Jonny and I gave a talk, 'It's an evolution neither of us saw coming.' In the beginning, every time we met again was exciting because of the way we were brought together. There was so much we were still keen to learn about each other. And yet, despite the many interviews we gave together after the reunion, it was a couple of months before we actually socialized. Since then, it's become a more organic friendship.

Sometimes a long period of time would pass before we saw each other. In fact, I hadn't heard much from Jonny in the two or three weeks leading up to his relapse in 2014. When I heard that he was back in hospital, I phoned Natasha, worried. She told me it might be best not to visit or call; for now only family were allowed. I wanted to reach out to him, but didn't think it was my place to do so. In the end I decided to text him. He replied that it would be best not to visit – he was very unwell.

At this point we had socialized a little, but most of our meetings had been work-related. I'd hoped that one day we would sit down and Jonny would open up to me. I guess I was waiting for some sort of revelation from him. I had expectations of a big conversation, closure maybe – a private opening rather than something for the media – but it never came. I realized at some point that it probably wasn't going to happen.

And yet, as I said, our friendship has evolved since then. I've always felt that he and I had a huge connection, and that we would have been friends if we'd met at school. We have very similar personalities. But as we work together closely these days, people want it to be still about that day, and my role in it. It's unique, and very special to me, and it's been a nice journey, but what's most important to me is the effect that Jonny has on the world. He is a truly incredible person. People ask why I stopped when hundreds of people walked past, but I just think I'm that kind of person.

I love our relationship, and I love Jonny.

Epilogue

Britt Pflüger

THE FIRST TIME I saw Jonny on breakfast television in 2014, talking about his search for the stranger who had talked him out of jumping from Waterloo Bridge six years earlier, I had no idea who he was. His story was incredibly moving, of course, but when he revealed that he had both schizoaffective disorder, a form of schizophrenia, as well inflammatory bowel disease, it really struck home: someone very close to me at the time had been diagnosed with schizoaffective disorder, and I myself have both Crohn's disease and severe depression. But what struck me most was the warmth and grace with which Jonny talked about what he had been through, and how determined he was to help others.

A newcomer to Twitter, I decided to follow him with no expectations of ever having any direct contact with him, and was delighted when he followed me back. I was just happy to read all about his journey and work as a mental-health campaigner, not least because recent events in my own life had opened my eyes to the shortcomings in mental-health services around the UK.

Being close to somebody with schizoaffective disorder can be incredibly challenging, especially when you receive little or no outside help, as I was soon to find out. In August that year, increasingly desperate and at my wits' end, I messaged Jonny via Twitter and asked for advice, not really expecting a response. By now he had well over 20,000 followers, and was no doubt inundated with messages, and yet he took the time to reply, offering invaluable advice and compassion. I remember how moved I was when he enquired after both our welfare as I was sitting in my friends' garden in Devon, our refuge at the time – ironically the very spot where we wrote much of this book almost three years later, ably assisted, or hindered, depending on your viewpoint, by sheepdogs Mickey and Molly.

Despite having worked in publishing for over twenty years, it would be another eighteen months before I approached Jonny with the idea of writing a book. This has often struck me as strange: surely that thought should have entered my mind straight away? In hindsight, being closely involved with someone who had schizo-affective disorder and little or no support from those around him, never mind the mental-health system, had given me blinders. My entire focus was on supporting my friend, to the point where I was neglecting my own mental health.

By now I had seen the brilliant Channel 4 documentary 'The Stranger on the Bridge' (and, like most people, I expect, sobbed my way through it), but it left me with a lot of questions; in particular, what took Jonny to the bridge that day and how had he managed to rebuild his life? So pressing was my curiosity that I approached him again on Twitter, suggesting coffee and a chat, once again not expecting a reply but getting one nonetheless. And that is how our journey started.

Jonny and I often talk about the line between mental illness and personality. Where does one end and the other start? How big a part does our upbringing play? Neither of us is a psychologist, but what I can say with absolute certainty is that Jonny's personality has played a vital part in his recovery, and in his determination to help others. I discovered later that when he messaged me on that sunny August day to find out how we were, he himself was becoming ill again, and yet there he was, worrying about complete strangers and making sure that they were OK. This is what makes Jonny so extraordinary. Through no fault of our own, often when we have a mental illness, we can become inward-looking, as all our energy is spent on day-to-day survival, sometimes to the point where we appear selfish to others. Jonny is the complete opposite: he is constantly caring for others, taking time to listen and trying to help, even when he is struggling himself. I don't think I have ever met anyone quite like him.

Now that we have become friends and I have got to know his warm and compassionate parents, this no longer surprises me. Kindness is something we often feel is lacking these days, but it is still very much around us if we care to look for it.

Kindness was certainly in the stranger who talked him down from the bridge that day.

Acknowledgements

I FEEL INCREDIBLY LUCKY to have such supportive family and friends. Whether it's a simple text from my brother to say 'hang in there', a card or letter from a friend who lives hundreds of miles away to tell me they are thinking of me, or a coffee with a colleague when I'm struggling to cope, I feel overwhelmed when I think of all the love and support I've received over the years.

During one stay in hospital my best friends sent me a VW Camper Van Lego set to keep me occupied. (I've always wanted a VW Camper Van!) I was so moved by this gesture. It certainly helped to move the endless hours in hospital along quicker!

Whenever I relapse now or say I'm struggling, the outpouring of kindness and encouragement I receive amazes me. Often I am truly touched by the words I am sent from strangers or acquaintances I have met online but never in person. As I may be unwell, I don't always respond to these messages but I certainly read them all and am so often inspired by them.

In my stubborn mind, I sometimes believe I can make this journey alone. But deep down in my heart I know I cannot, and I truly need the help of others along this bumpy, winding road called life.

Endnotes and Resources

1 According to a BBC News online article from January 2017, the number of patients going to A&E with psychiatric issues rose by 50 per cent between 2011 and 2016. 'Steep Rise in A&E Psychiatric Patients', http://www.bbc.co.uk/news/health-38576368, accessed January 2018

2 Police suspect a dramatic increase in their use of emergency powers to deal with people suffering a mental-health crisis is because of cuts to community psychiatric care. The number of instances of section 136 powers (when the police have to talk someone down from a building or bridge or come across someone agitated in the street) having to be implemented increased to 28,271 in 2015, up from 17,417 in 2005–6. Alex Marshall, head of the College of Policing, said: 'This is a real live issue in all parts of the country. People in a mental-health crisis should receive support, whatever time of day or night, from a properly trained mental health professional.' The lead on mental-health issues for the College of Policing, Inspector Michael Brown, told the *Guardian*: 'Police are relied on as an emergency crisis service more now than previously. The police are using the power more. This may be attributable to some areas not having enough availability to care for people in the community, as opposed to in mental health hospitals and units.' *Guardian* online article, 9 October 2016: 'Police Say They Are Becoming Emergency Mental Health Services', https://www.theguardian.com/uk-news/2016/oct/09/police-forces-mental-health-section-136, accessed January 2018

3 According to an article in the *Independent* from 6 December 2015, the results from Finland over the past thirty years are impressive.

Not only were 74 per cent of patients experiencing psychosis back at work within two years, compared with just 9 per cent in the UK at the time, but suicide rates were significantly lower: 'Here, a mental-health diagnosis can feel like a life sentence' Celia Dodd, the *Independent,* 6 December 2015, http://www.independent.co.uk/life-style/health-and-families/health-news/open-dialogue-the-radical-new-treatment-having-life-changing-effects-on-peoples-mental-health-a6762391.html, accessed November 2017

4 Jamie Doward, 'Children's tsar savages NHS over "unacceptable" mental health care', the *Observer,* 15 October 2017, https://www.theguardian.com/society/2017/oct/14/childrens-commissioner-attacks-nhs-mental-health, accessed November 2017

5 National Audit Office, 'Mental Health in Prisons', www.nao.org.uk/report/mental-health-in-prisons/, accessed January 2018

6 National Audit Office, 'Mental Health in Prisons', www.nao.org.uk/report/mental-health-in-prisons/, accessed January 2018

7 Karen McVeigh, 'Fit for work assessment was trigger for suicide, coroner says', the *Guardian,* 21 September 2015, https://www.theguardian.com/politics/2015/sep/21/fit-for-work-assessment-was-trigger-for-suicide-coroner-says, accessed November 2017

8 John Pring, 'Michael O'Sullivan scandal: DWP twice pushed dad-of-two to suicide bids', 23 October 2015, https://www.disabilitynewsservice.com/michael-osullivan-scandal-dwp-twice-pushed-dad-of-two-to-suicide-bids, accessed November 2017

9 ITV News online article, 14 April 2017, 'DWP "rewarding failure" With Benefit Assessors Payouts', http://www.itv.com/news/2017-04-14/dwp-rewarding-failure-with-benefit-assessors-payouts/, accessed January 2018

10 ITV News online article, 14 April 2017, 'DWP "rewarding failure" With Benefit Assessors Payouts', http://www.itv.com/news/2017-04-14/dwp-rewarding-failure-with-benefit-assessors-payouts/, accessed January 2018

11 Jon Stone, 'DWP's fit-to-work tests "cause permanent damage to mental health", study finds', 13 March 2017, http://www.

independent.co.uk/news/uk/politics/fit-to-work-wca-tests-mental-health-dwp-work-capability-assessment-benefits-esa-pip-a7623686.html, accessed November 2017

12 Oliver Wright, 'DWP fit-to-work assessments cost more money than they save, report reveals', 8 January 2016, http://www.independent.co.uk/news/uk/politics/dwp-fit-to-work-assessments-cost-more-than-they-save-report-reveals-a6801636.html, accessed November 2017.

Resources

Support

Amy Winehouse Foundation, drug and alcohol misuse charity set up in memory of the late singer, http://amywinehousefoundation.org/

Balanced Minds, Centre for Compassion-Focused Therapy, http://balancedminds.com/

CALM, The Campaign Against Living Miserably, https://www.thecalmzone.net/

Centre For Mental Health, the mental-health research, policy and service provision charity, https://www.centreformentalhealth.org.uk/

Charlie Waller Memorial Trust, educates and raises awareness on mental health & wellbeing by delivering talks to young people, teachers and parents, https://www.cwmt.org.uk/

Crohn's and Colitis UK, https://www.crohnsandcolitis.org.uk/about-inflammatory-bowel-disease/crohns-disease, Information service (including disability benefits and parent to parent service) 0300 222 5700 (Mon, Tues, Wed & Fri: 9 a.m. to 5 p.m., Thur: 9 a.m. to 1 p.m.); Crohn's & Colitis Support 0121 737 9931 (1 p.m. to 3.30 p.m. Tues to Thur; 6.30 p.m. to 9 p.m. Mon to Fri), email info@crohnsandcolitis.org.uk

Dr Charlie Heriot-Maitland, Balanced Minds (compassion-focused therapy based in London and Edinburgh), http://balancedminds.com, email london@balancedminds.com, edinburgh@balancedminds.com

Dr Kristin Neff, Self-Compassion (compassion-focused therapy based in the USA), http://self-compassion.org, email selfcompassion. questions@gmail.com

Heads Together, https://www.headstogether.org.uk

Headmeds, mental-health medication information website, https:// www.headmeds.org.uk/

Hub of Hope, national mental-health database, https://hubofhope. co.uk/

If U Care Share, Supporting families affected by suicide, https://www. ifucareshare.co.uk, 0191 387 5661, email share@ifucareshare.co.uk

JAMI, The Mental Health Charity for the Jewish Community, http:// jamiuk.org/

Maudsley Charity, Health in Mind, http://www.maudsleycharity.org, 020 3696 9760

MIND, for better mental health, mind.org.uk, infoline call 0300 123 3393 or text 86463. Mind provides a list of crisis services at https:// www.mind.org.uk

MindOut, mental-health charity for the LGBTQ community, https:// www.mindout.org.uk/

Maytree, A Sanctuary for the Suicidal, http://maytree.org.uk, 020 7263 7070

Mental Health Mates, http://mentalhealthmates.co.uk

Mental Health Foundation, provides information, carries out research, and campaigns to improve services for people affected by mental-health problems https://www.mentalhealth.org.uk/

MQ, Transforming Mental Health Through Research https://www. mqmentalhealth.org/

Nightline Association, mental-health support service for university students, https://www.nightline.ac.uk/

NSPA, The National Suicide Prevention Alliance, http://www.nspa.org. uk/

Place2Be, providing in-school counselling support and expert training to improve the emotional wellbeing of pupils, families, and teachers, https://www.place2be.org.uk/

Rethink Mental Illness, https://www.rethink.org, General Enquiries

and Supporter Care 0121 522 7007, Rethink Advice and Information
Service 0300 5000 927

Royal College of Psychiatrists, professional body responsible for
education and training, and setting and raising standards in
psychiatry, http://www.rcpsych.ac.uk/

Samaritans, https://www.samaritans.org, 116 123 (UK), 116 123 (ROI),
free call; email jo@samaritans.org

SANE, charity improving quality of life for anyone affected by mental
illness – including family friends and carers, http://www.sane.org.uk/

Snehalaya, NGO in India that provides services to women, children and
LGBT communities affected by HIV, AIDS, poverty, violence and sex
trafficking, http://www.snehalaya.org/

SOBS (Survivors of Bereavement by Suicide), https://uksobs.org, 0300
111 5065 (9 a.m.–9 p.m. daily), email sobs.support@hotmail.com

St Mungo's, Ending homelessness, Rebuilding lives, https://www.
mungos.org, 020 3856 6000, email info@mungos.org (reply within
two working days)

Time to Change, https://www.time-to-change.org.uk

The Alchemy Project, A dance-led intervention for young adults living
with psychosis, http://www.aesopmarketplace.org/arts-programmes/
alchemy-project

The Landmark Forum, http://landmarkforum.com

The What If Academy, a ground-breaking social enterprise dedicated to
bringing personal development programmes to young people, http://
www.whatifacademy.org.uk/

ThinkWell mental-health workshop, Pixel Learning, https://www.
pixellearning.org/

Young Minds, the UK's leading charity committed to improving the
wellbeing and mental health of young people, https://youngminds.
org.uk/

Books and CDs
Mindfulness: A Practical Guide to Finding Peace in a Frantic World by
Mark Williams and Danny Penman (Piatkus, 2011)

Mindfulness for Beginners, CD by Jon Kabat-Zinn, the founder of
MBSR (Mindfulness-Based Stress Reduction)

Pill After Pill: Poems From A Schizophrenic Mind by Jonathan
Benjamin (Chipmunka Publishing, 2012)

Self Compassion: stop beating yourself up and leave insecurity behind
by Kristin Neff (Yellow Kite, 2011)

The Little CBT Workbook by Dr Michael Sinclair and Dr Belinda
Hollingsworth (Crimson Publishing, 2012)

Retreats

Hoffman Process, renowned week-long personal development retreat,
https://www.hoffmaninstitute.co.uk/

The Sharpham Trust, Ashprington, Totnes, Devon, TQ9 7UT, http://
www.sharphamtrust.org, 01803 732542

Wilderness Minds, mindfulness meditation in the wild through guided
mountain walks, sea kayaking, camping and trekking, http://
wildernessminds.co.uk/

Apps

Doc Ready, http://www.docready.org

Elefriends, online mental-health community, https://www.elefriends.
org.uk/

Insight Timer, meditation app, https://insighttimer.com/

Unmind, wellness app for organizations, http://unmind.com/

Videos and vlogs

'The voices in my head', TED talk by Eleanor Longden, https://www.
ted.com/talks/eleanor_longden_the_voices_in_my_head

Jonny Benjamin YouTube channel: www.youtube.com/johnjusthuman

Jonny Benjamin

JONNY IS AN AWARD-WINNING mental health campaigner, film producer, public speaker, writer and vlogger. In 2017, Jonny was recognised for his work as an influential activist changing the culture around mental health, when he was awarded an MBE in the Queen's New Year's Honours List. At the age of 20 he was diagnosed with schizoaffective disorder, a combination of schizophrenia and bipolar, and later began making films on YouTube about the condition that have since been watched by hundreds of thousands of people. Jonny now speaks publicly about living with mental illness and has written articles and given various interviews on TV, radio and in print around the world to help educate and break stigma.

Britt Pflüger

BRITT IS A LITERARY CONSULTANT with over 25 years' experience in publishing. She was born in Germany and has lived and worked in the UK since graduating from King's College London.